SACRED S

IN SEARCH OF
THE HOLY WELLS AND SPAS OF WALES

Paul Davis

First published 2003

ISBN 1 872730 30 2

BLORENGE BOOKS

Blorenge Cottage, Church Lane, Llanfoist, Abergavenny, Gwent NP7 9NG
Tel: 01873 856114

Printed by Mid Wales Print Group,
Units 10/13, Pontyfelin Industrial Estate, New Inn,
Pontypool, Torfaen NP4 ODQ
Tel: 01495 750033

Front Cover: St Mary's Well, Penrhys

Back Cover: St Winifride's Well, Holywell

CONTENTS

Higgon's Well, Haverfordwest

INTRODUCTION

'For the itch and the stitch, Rheumatic and the gout,
If the Devil isn't in you, the well will take them out'
- An old Glamorgan rhyme.

Mention the word 'well' and the first image that probably comes to mind is that familiar garden ornamental of a circular pit topped with a cupola and windlass. But for centuries the word has been used to describe natural springs (ffynnon in Welsh) rather than man-made boreholes. Today, water flows in our homes at the turn of a tap, and it is only during exceptional droughts (or when you don't pay the bill) that we appreciate its value. How much more important then, for our ancestors without modern facilities, to have a ready source of water to hand? For centuries, people have visited certain wells and springs renowned for their healing properties, and although this practice has a certain veneer of Christianity, the beliefs originated long before the first saints and holy men set foot in Britain.

The essential starting point for anyone researching this subject is Francis Jones's book, *The Holy Wells of Wales*, first published in 1954, and reissued recently. Jones spent years trawling through libraries, antiquarian journals and archives, to produce the definitive source-book on the subject. But this, alas, is the main problem with the book; it is a purely academic work, and there is little evidence that the author spent any time 'in the field' finding out what -if anything- survived in his day. Furthermore, no adequate directions or grid references were provided for plotting sites onto modern Ordnance Survey (OS) maps. In the intervening years, so much has changed in the rural landscape that many of these wells can no longer be found. This book therefore intends to correct that lapse - or at least provide a stop-gap in advance of any future, detailed survey of Welsh holy wells.

Pre-Christian water cults

'Water fell there in abundance from dark springs'

Lucan, on Druid shrines, Pharsalia (first century AD)

Water is a prerequisite of life, and its availability was essential for the location and survival of any habitation in early times. The very image of a strong supply of pure, clean water, bursting out of the ground or a rock outcrop, has a near-magical quality; it is no wonder that our ancestors worshipped springs, wells and water sources as aspects of nature deities. The Celtic tribes of the Iron Age (c500 BC - 100 AD) are known to have offered gifts of precious metal to the gods of lakes and rivers. Excavations at Llyn Cerrig Bach (Anglesey) and Llyn Fawr (Rhondda) have uncovered a wealth of tools, weapons, and other implements. They also venerated the head as the seat of human knowledge and power, and not only collected skulls as trophies and heirlooms, but introduced the gory image to their art and iconography. It is from this pre-Roman period that the enduring traditions of throwing a votive offering into a well (whether it be a coin, pin, or pebble) originated. And the legends of springs miraculously appearing at the decapitation of a saint must surely recall the older, pre-Christian beliefs and rituals of the Celts. Carved stone heads have been found in north-west Wales (particularly Anglesey, last stronghold of the Druids), and at Tremeirchion, Llanmihangel, and Garthbeibio, stone heads and human figures have been recorded at the actual wells. Even in relatively recent days people would drink healing water out of a human skull at Ffynnon Deilo (Maenclochog). More remarkably, there may be a rare survivor of a pre-Christian shrine at Tarren Ddeusant, in a remote valley near Cardiff. Although marked on some old maps as a 'well' there is only a boggy patch here, fed by water dripping from overhanging crags. But carved into the rock beside a phallic boulder are a number of human heads, two of which bear a marked similarity to the mysterious, haunting faces of Celtic art.

The spread of Christianity, and the Middle Ages

'A new myth for an old rite has often been a device of priests and potentates'

H J Fleure, A Natural History of Man in Britain (1951)

The long-held beliefs of the Celts were too deeply rooted to be totally superseded by the new religion of the Early Christian missionaries. In a

Mysterious Celtic faces adorn the rocks at Tarren Ddeusant

famous letter written in 601 by Pope Gregory, concerning St Augustine's mission to Britain, he instructed that the pagan idols should be destroyed, but their temples ought to be converted to Christian use. That way the people would still frequent their familiar places of worship, but would henceforth pray to the one true God. By the time Augustine preached to the pagan Saxons, Celtic saints and holy men had long been at work in Wales. Men like Dewi, Teilo, Illtud, Beuno and their followers, spread the gospel throughout the land from monastic centres and simple religious outposts. There are over 200 churches and chapels built close to wells and Prehistoric stone monuments, perhaps in a conscious attempt to sanctify pagan sites. However, it is impossible to prove that every spring was sacred to pre-Christian people, and the siting of a chapel close to a viable water supply may have been a simple human necessity. Nevertheless, over the years such springs have invariably assumed the status of a 'holy' well, usually bearing the name of a saint, and boasting curative properties.

Many of the churches and shrines were controlled by the great monastic houses, and were deliberately cultivated as places of pilgrimage. Two journeys to St Davids Cathedral were considered to be the equal of one to Rome, and along the main routes there were chapels and religious shrines eager to offer spiritual well-being and hospitality, in return for the coins of the devout traveller. Other notable places of pilgrimage in Wales include Bardsey Island (Lleyn), Penrhys (Rhondda), and the famous shrine of St Winefride at Holywell. It was not only the magical qualities of sacred springs that drew and sustained pilgrims on their arduous trek; several churches had the extra pulling-power of miraculous effigies or saintly relics, such as the wooden statue of Derfel Gadarn at Llandderfel, and the tombs of St Beuno at Clynnog Fawr and St Melangell at Pennant Melangell. The financial contributions swelled the coffers of the clergy and edified buildings up and down the country. The later Middle Ages witnessed a renaissance in church architecture, and we have the coins of pilgrims to thank for the fine Perpendicular churches at Clynnog and Holywell; the beautiful stained glass window at Llanrhaeadr; and the smaller chapels at Ffynnon Fair (Trefnant), Llanddwyn Island, and St Justinians (St Davids).

Clynnog Fawr was built in the 16th century on the site of a much older shrine

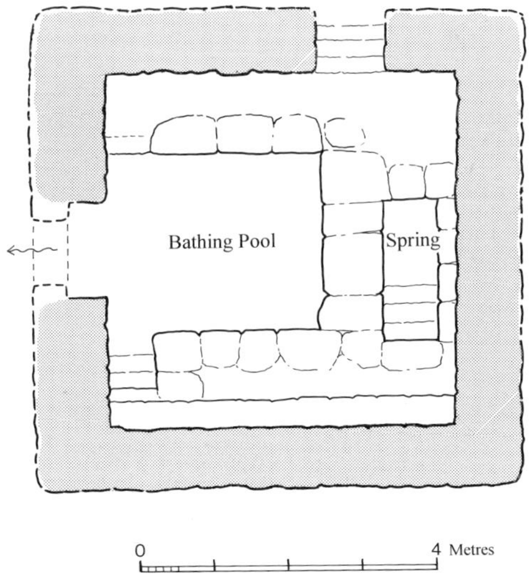

Mynytho (Lleyn): Plan of Ffynnon Fyw

Healing powers of the wells

'And after the hede of the Vyrgyne was cut of and touchyd the ground... sprang up a welle of spryngyng water largely enduryng unto this day, which heleth al langours and sekenesses' -

Caxton, The Life of St Winefride (1485)

It is easy for us today to sneer cynically at the rapacious greed of some churchmen, eager to cash in on pilgrims by offering cures and 'holy' relics for a price; but there can be no doubt that faith was responsible for many small miracles. Until comparatively recently, life for the majority of people was very simple, very harsh, and very short. Infant mortality was commonplace, and few people lived their allotted three score years and ten. Before the discovery of penicillin and paracetamol, sick people either had to endure their afflictions, or seek help through what today might be called herbal medicine. The benefits of pure cold water, blessed by saintly powers, and sometimes tinged with minerals dissolved from underground strata, was considered sufficient to elicit cures.

For centuries people sought relief from a staggering variety of illnesses, of which the most commonplace were rheumatism, sore eyes, sprained or broken limbs, bladder stones, eczema, warts and scrofula (also known as King's Evil - a tubercular infection of the lymph glands). A few wells were even reputed to cure more serious illnesses such as cancer, epilepsy and paralysis. The rituals involved in the healing process were just as varied. Sometimes a pilgrim need only drink, or wash in the water, to receive better health, and a votive offering such as a quartz pebble or a bent pin, would be thrown in. For warts and skin diseases it was usually necessary to rub the infected part with a rag dipped in the water, and then hang the cloth on a nearby bush. The reasoning behind this was that the disease would be 'passed on' to the rag (or a pin if used instead), and it was important that no-one touched the rag or the warts would be 'transferred' to that person. This simple ritual might have to be carried out at a certain time of the day, or even on a particular day of the year. But sometimes a far more complex procedure was needed to effect a result, which might include pagan rituals, reciting poems or rhymes, and even sleeping overnight on stone slabs (see the gazetteer entries on Llandegla, Llangybi, & Clynnog Fawr). The treatment might continue for several days, even weeks. Sometimes the well was 'consulted' to foretell the future, to find out if a lover would be faithful, or just visited to make a simple wish. A few had a much darker reputation for bringing bad luck on someone. The most famous -or rather infamous- member of this category was at Llanelian in the mountains above Colwyn Bay. Although no longer in existence, the dreadful reputation of Ffynnon Elian as a 'cursing well' stretches across the centuries.

All springs are naturally occurring geological features, but since imagination was in use long before scientific reason, many remarkable legends have evolved to explain their origin. Francis Jones recorded over 400 wells named after saints, and many were reputedly formed at the command of a holy man to prove the power and authority of God. Just as Moses produced water by striking his staff against a rock, so St Cybi (among many others) repeated the miracle to bring forth Ffynnon Gybi in Lleyn. As late as 1867 the same basic story was told of a spring at Llandrindod, which was supposedly discovered when someone hit a tent peg in the ground!

Ffynnon Gybi in Lleyn (Chris Barber)

There is clearly a biblical origin for such tales, but another branch of well lore derives from the pre-Roman Celtic head cult. The most famous is, of course, the legend of Gwenfrewi, or St Winefride, who was beheaded by a lustful admirer, and where her head fell to the ground, a powerful spring gushed out. St Decuman and St Justinian actually picked up their heads and walked across the sea, before coming to rest on the mainland where springs welled up. Certain lakes are supposed to have been formed when someone forgot to put the lid back on a well, to prevent widespread flooding. This is told of Llyn Llech Owen (Llandybie), Ffynnon Gower (Bala) and Ffynnon Grassi (Lleyn). Such tales are explored in depth by Sir John Rhys in Celtic Folklore (1901), and it should be remembered that these legends are not only restricted to Wales; they are associated with holy wells and sacred springs all over Britain.

The Reformation

'And in view of the claim that the water is medicinal appoint two men to test its properties; if not medicinal the well should be destroyed.'

Elizabeth I to the Council of the Marches, concerning Holywell (1579)

Henry VIII's break with Rome in the 1530's signalled the closure of the great monasteries and all the establishments dependant on them. The effects of the Reformation was felt across the land, and experienced by all levels of society. Pilgrimages to Catholic shrines were forbidden, and the images and buildings which had attracted the worship and offerings of the devout, were destroyed. Without the financial backing of contributions from pilgrims and wealthy patrons, hundreds of small rural chapels fell into ruin. A few like St Non's Chapel (St Davids), Capel Erbach (Porthyrhyd), & Ffynnon Fair (Trefnant), have managed to survive in some tangible form to the present day, but many others are now commemorated only by insignificant earthworks or place-name evidence. Despite the brief reversal during the reign of Queen Mary, the Protestant faith held sway, and the authorities harshly clamped down on any 'superstitious' practices.

The high-profile monastic establishments never rose from the ashes, and yet it proved more difficult for the iconoclasts to wholly erase the beliefs and customs associated with the less conspicuous holy well. Throughout the sixteenth century there are numerous records of unofficial pilgrimages to wells that the authorities appear unable (or unwilling) to stop. That the great shrine of Holywell is with us today is nothing short of a miracle in itself. St Meugan's chapel (Eglwyswrw) was just one of the many casualties of the age. Royal agents were appointed to wreck the shrine and not leave one stone upon another, and if anyone attempted a bit of furtive rebuilding, they were to be arrested. The absence of any structure here today (other than the still flowing spring) is proof of the agents' thoroughness.

In 1590 it was written that the Welsh people *'doe still goe in heapes one pilgrimage to the wanted welles and places of superstition'*. While in 1594 up to 200 people at a time were visiting Ffynnon Gwyddfan at Llandyfan. Those arrested were later released by a sympathetic magistrate who decided that they were just poor people taking the water to be cured of their illnesses with God's help. A few years before this event, Queen Elizabeth requested the Council of the Marches to send two agents to Holywell to test the properties of the water there, with the proviso that 'if not medicinal the Well should be destroyed' This is the clue to the continued survival of the water cult into the present day. The old traditions were too deeply rooted to be shaken off, and just as the first Christians had adopted pagan beliefs and places of worship for their own ends, so the Protestants further modified the age-old pilgrimage ritual to water shrines. The age of the spa had arrived.

Holywell (Chris Barber)

The Welsh Spa

'Full oft have I repaired to drink that spring, waters which cure diseases of the soul as well as body'

Lewis Morris (1701-1765) on St Gwenfaen's Well

The fundamental difference between a spa and a holy well is essentially one of religious faith. Spring water was still believed to cure various illnesses, but now the reason for the cure was not down to the magical healing powers of the titular saint, but due to the mineral content of the water. A spa is the realm of the scientist and quack medic, not the cleric and saintly hermit.

Spa water is valued upon the minerals it contains. As rainwater slowly percolates through the rocks deep underground, minerals are dissolved from the surrounding strata, producing distinctive tasting (and smelling!) water. The water that emerged from Taff's Well had passed so far underground, that it had been warmed up by natural geothermal heat. Most spas had chalybeate water (containing iron oxide) and sulphur waters (hydrogen sulphide) on tap.

Despite stories of Roman origins for the springs at Taff's Well, Trefriw and Llandrindod, the heyday of the Welsh spas extended from the mid-eighteenth to the late-nineteenth centuries, - but commercial success was never assured and, ultimately, the sea-side holiday won the affection of the British public. The origins of the spas are to be found in the changing attitudes to holy wells prevalent in the sixteenth and seventeenth centuries. Some of the older sacred springs gained a new lease of life, such as Llangybi (Lleyn), where a cottage was added to one side of the older well; and Llanrhaeadr, which was graced with ornamental statues and changing rooms. The most famous Welsh spa was **Llandrindod Wells**, and the present townscape of red brick houses and decorative cast-iron verandas is a legacy of the Victorian craze for health resorts. The medicinal value of a chalybeate spring called Ffynnon Llwyn-y-gog (Cuckoo grove well), was noted in 1696, but development of the spa only took off in the 1730's. A large house below the old church was converted into *'a spacious hotel, capable of accommodating numerous families'*, and incorporated shops, billiard room, and a ballroom under one roof. So popular was the venue that The Gentlemenís Magazine of 1748 proclaimed *'Let England boast Bath's crowded springs, Llandrindod happier, Cambria sings'*. A few years later Dr Wessel Linden was cured of a skin complaint and put the spa firmly on the tourist map with the publication of his *Treatise on the Three Medicinal Mineral Waters of Llandrindod* (1756). The hotel was so crowded in the summer season that some guests had to stay in Builth Wells. But the ebullient antics of the well-to-do water drinkers annoyed the authorities to such an extent (*'a gambling and whoring hell'* they cried) that the hotel was closed in 1787.

The revival came with the Regency period in the early nineteenth century, and the new Pump House and Rock House hotels opened their doors for trade. The three waters mentioned by Linden were saline, chalybeate, and sulphur; and Samuel Lewis (who compiled a *Topographical Dictionary of Wales* in the 1830's) recommended they be drunk 'early in the morning, on an empty stomach'. The various illnesses treated included skin problems, liver complaints, indigestion, rheumatism, gout, scrofula, ulcers and bladder diseases. Trade had declined by the middle of the century, as the fickle customers took to the sea, but the arrival of the Central Wales Railway in the 1860's initiated the final boom. The whole town was virtually rebuilt; grander hotels sprang up, and a new bath and pump house was built at the Rock House in 1872. In 1871 the population was 350, and by 1899 this had more than quadrupled to 1624.

The fastidious Victorians drank, tested, and eulogised the various mineral waters to their hearts content. T.R. Robert's book *The Spas of Wales* (1897) provided readers with detailed analysis of the chemical composition of the springs, and the methods of taking them (in some cases just as elaborate as a holy well ritual). Three to five glasses should be sipped in the morning only, followed by a brisk walk. Lewis' coy instructions were swept away by Robert's bluff advice; *'If the water agrees with the patient, a free, copious and painless action of the bowels follows; breakfast-time is awaited with eagerness, the dull and leaden eye becomes bright and sparkling... flatulence disappears... and tranquil and refreshing sleep is obtained'*.

The lure of the sea-side again signalled the end of the inland spa in the first half of the twentieth century, but at least the visible heritage of those days is plain to see at Llandrindod. The Pump House still stands beside the Ithon brook below the town, and built into the wall beside the path is a stone spout giving a free supply of the iron-rich waters that drew all and sundry here.

Mid Wales gave birth to a number of other spas in the wake of Llandrindod's success. In 1732 The Rev Theophilus Evans visited a foul-smelling sulphur spring at **Llanwrtyd** in the Irfon valley in the hope of a cure for his skin disease. He was at first highly reluctant to test the water, but on seeing a perfectly healthy-looking frog jump out, decided to try his luck. After two months of drinking and washing in the spring, he was cured, and Llanwrtyd was on its way to becoming another successful spa. The spring was called Ffynnon Drewllyd ('stinking well'), but this was changed to the more musical sounding Dol-y-coed, and the waters were diverted into a nearby bath house. Samuel Lewis wrote *'it is now much resorted to in the Summer season, and a comfortable mansion... is open for the public accommodation; with conveniences for warm and cold bathing'*. The quality of the water was compared favourably with the better-known sulphur spa at Harrogate in Yorkshire.

A somewhat similar story is told about the discovery of a barrium chloride spring at **Llangammarch**. Around 1837 a local farmer went in search of a lost pig and found the animal cooling itself in a muddy spring in the dried-up bed of the Irfon. He first thought the unpleasant tasting water was poisonous, and tried to prevent it from fouling the local supply. However, the medicinal value of the spring was soon recognised, and a pump-house was set up to bring a supply to the nearby Lake Hotel. Barrium water was considered good for the heart, and was taken internally and externally. The crumbling ruins of the little pump-house with its adjoining open-air pool can still be seen on the riverbank below the hotel, about 1km north-east of the village.

Further down river at **Builth**, the chalybeate and sulphur springs were a poorer alternative to Llandrindod, but visitors from far afield still made the journey. The poet Lewis Morris from Anglesey wrote that the waters were *'Good for asthmas and diseases of ye Lungs, consumptions &c. It tastes strong of sulpher and smells much like gunpowder'* (1748).

At Park Wells (Builth Wells) the octagonal pump house still survives

There were two spas at Builth, offering customers a choice of saline, chalybeate and sulphur waters. Glannau Wells lies 1km west of the town in the middle of the new golf course, just off the road to Llanwrtyd. Here in the woods stood a timber pavilion and a rather grim looking two-storey stone pump house. Park Wells lies further north, beside a minor road from the clubhouse to Comin Coch. Water was drawn from a pump housed in an attractive, octagonal building with a peaked roof. The *Cambrian Travellers Guide* of 1813 noted that the first floor was *'a neat and commodious apartment in which the visitors occasionally amuse themselves with dancing'*. A timber framed pavilion was later added nearby. Although both buildings still survive, they are no longer used, but can be seen from a public foot-path bordering the drive to Park Wells house. The medical qualities of Builth water was just as efficacious as the other spas (and *'very useful as an injection for piles'* wrote one satisfied customer in 1896), but the town never posed a serious rival to Llandrindod. Lack of adequate accommodation was an oft-repeated complaint, and the class of clientele was not always satisfactory. Visitors in 1903 were rather snootily advised to *'avoid the actual holiday season'* when the town was invaded by *'the Joes and Jills of the Glamorgan collieries, who flock hither to drink the most potent saline water that the heart of a dyspeptic could desire'*!

Trefriw was something of a late starter, and lies far to the north on the banks of the Conwy. A mining agent scouting for new locations discovered the spring in 1833, and a bath house was opened in the 1860's. According to T. R. Roberts the Trefriw spa season lasted from late April to late September, and the water was considered good for treating *'melancholia, hypochondriacism... indigestion, dyspepsia, chronic jaundice'*. Trade dwindled away in the 1930's when steamer trips upriver from Conwy town were cancelled, and the spa soon closed. However, Trefriw has recently gained a new lease of life, and the iron-rich water is available commercially.

The popularity of the major spas led numerous entrepreneurs to jump on the bandwagon and exploit a handy spring. Samuel Lewis made reference to many such establishments in his *Topographical Dictionary of Wales*, but few lasted long, or left any tangible mark on the landscape. Two are worth highlighting here. Near Glascwm (Powys) Thomas Frankland diverted the sulphur waters of Blaen-edwy into a bath-house, and converted a nearby farm into a small hotel. According to Lewis the springs were popular, *'but the scarcity of lodgings, and the dreary and uninteresting character of the surrounding scenery, operates powerfully to retard their rising importance'*. Further south, in the fertile Vale of Tywi, Sir William Paxton was carrying out improvements to Middleton Hall (now the site of the National Botanic Garden of Wales). Chalybeate springs in the grounds were analysed and considered to be *'similar to the Tunbridge waters, except that they hold in solution a larger proportion of iron and are therefore more powerful'*. Lewis mentions that hot and cold bath-houses had been built near them, but now only a modern 'holy well' remains at the Pont Felin-gat picnic area. Many wealthy landowners with extensive properties had bath-houses as a feature of their landscaped gardens. The buildings sometimes resembled holy wells, but usually relied on a nearby stream or ornamental lake for a water source, and so are outside the scope of this book. Other examples of briefly famous spas include Clawdd-llesg (Meifod), Garthmaelwg (Llantrisant), Llandegley, Newbridge-on-Wye, and Taffs Well. Some are mentioned in the gazetteer section, but many others are commemorated only by the spring itself, or the crumbling remains of bath-houses and changing rooms - as much an architectural curiosity as the holy wells of the Middle Ages.

The architecture of holy wells

'It is now in contemplation to enclose the springs and to erect a small pump-room, with other appendages, for the accommodation of visitors'

Samuel Lewis on Gumfreston, *Topographical Dictionary of Wales* (1833)

Francis Jones listed almost 1200 holy wells in Wales, but only a small number have any structure or building associated with them. There are even fewer sites which can be fairly accurately dated. The most common and simplest form of well-building is an arrangement of stone slabs, or a low wall, around the head of the spring itself, such as can be seen at Dolwyddelan, Glasbury, Gumfreston, Llanallgo, Llandegla, and Llangybi. Sometimes this open pool arrangement is quite large and well built, with a surrounding wall and steps going down into the water, as at Bryncroes, Cilcain, Clynnog Fawr, Derwen, Llandyfan, Llanfair Caereinion, Llangybi (Lleyn), Mold, and Trellech.

A small number of wells are almost completely enclosed with masonry, usually in the form of a vaulted hood, as at St Non's chapel, Llangynhafal, Llanllawer, Swyddffynnon and Wilcrick; while at Llanddew, Llangadfan, Llansteffan, Patrishow and Cwm, the springs rise within wall recesses. There are also a handful of substantial stone buildings which form the most impressive holy wells in Wales. The vaulted cells at Penrhys, Brecon, Margam, Penmon and Haverfordwest, are relatively small and functioned purely to enclose and protect the water supply; but the larger buildings at St Govan's Chapel, Capel Erbach, Capel Trillo and Ffynnon

Fair, fulfilled a dual role as well-chapels. Greatest of all is the combined well and chapel-shrine of St Winefride at Holywell, a product of the last, glorious flowering of Medieval art.

How old are the wells? With the right geological conditions springs can flow uninterrupted for thousands of years, and there is no reason to doubt that people have utilised and venerated certain water sources since Prehistoric times. The presence of memorial stones at many church and well sites (Llangybi, Llanaelhearn, Llanllawer, and Maenclochog, for instance) indicates that Early Christian missionaries were active in certain areas during the Dark Ages. However, it seems unlikely that any structure remaining at a well today could date from such a distant period. Many certainly look crude enough to be ancient, but they could equally be relatively modern, and simply the result of unskilled rebuilding work carried out every few generations.

Unlike castles and abbeys, holy wells do not have a convenient chronological cut-off point, since pilgrimages (of one sort or another) continued until fairly recent times. Furthermore, the majority of well buildings have no dateable architectural features. Some of the larger buildings can be broadly dated; St Govans chapel has been variously ascribed to the thirteenth or fifteenth centuries; Capel Erbach and Capel Begawdin are probably early fourteenth century, and Holywell, along with Ffynnon Fair, was built around 1500. The square pool at Clynnog Fawr is perhaps contemporary with the early-sixteenth century rebuilding of the church, and the vaulted cell at Penrhys may predate the closure of the pilgrimage centre in 1536.

St Mary's Well, Penrhys

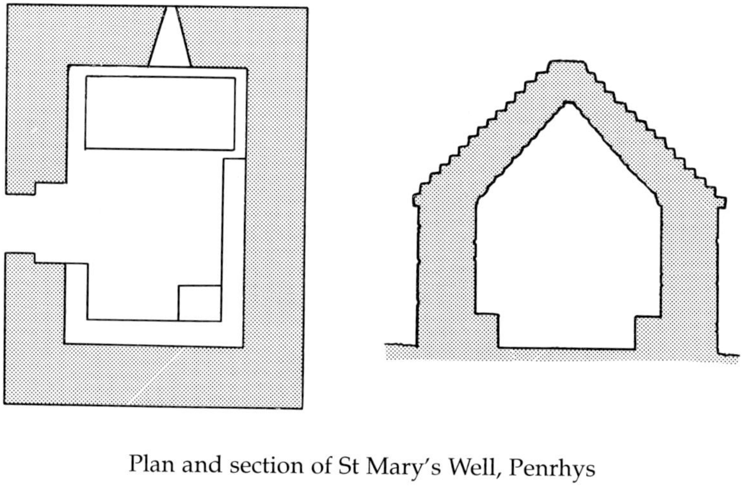

Plan and section of St Mary's Well, Penrhys

The wells at Brecon Cathedral, Gwaunysgor, Llanmihangel and Tremeirchion incorporate reused Medieval stonework, and so must be post-Reformation. Mathern and Trelleck are probably seventeenth century. Of course the danger of attempting to date an undateable building is highlighted by Maen-du well in Brecon, which is a splendid little vaulted cell reminiscent of Early Christian chapels in Ireland and Scotland. A datestone by the entrance reveals it was actually built in 1754!

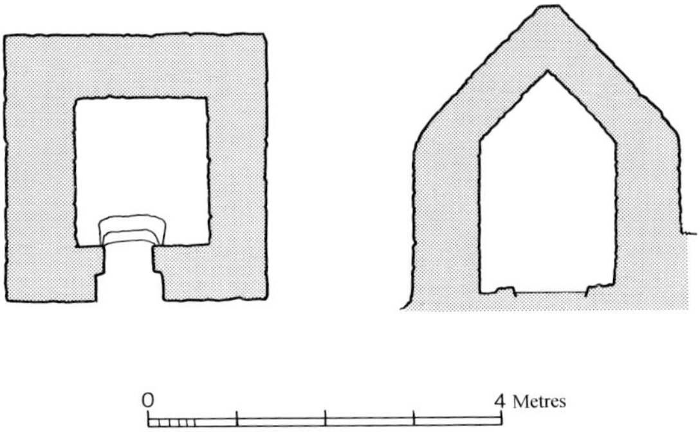

Plan and section of Maen-du, Brecon

The future

'Local memory of many holy-well sites is fading and... the above ground remains of many need recording before their location is forgotten.'

Nancy Edwards *The Archaeology of Clwyd* (1991)

As society bustles into the new millennium, many small and comparatively insignificant archaeological monuments are at risk from creeping urbanisation, new road networks, intensified agriculture and - perhaps worse of all- indifference and neglect. In the early years of the twentieth century the Royal Commission on Ancient and Historical Monuments for Wales (RCAHMW) published a series of county *inventories* which included many holy wells that were still being visited for spiritual or medicinal purposes. By the time Francis Jones published his *magnum opus* in 1954 many of these traditions had been forgotten, and the wells themselves viewed more as a convenient water source than an integral part of rural life. No more would people gather in the fields around a well, on a Sunday or holy day, to drink sweetened water, play games, and celebrate the simple joys of living. The countryside and farming practices have changed considerably since Jones'day, and now only a fraction of the hundreds of wells survive. Very few are still named and marked on OS maps; worse still, certain sites -Ffynnon Gredifael (Anglesey), and Ffynnon Faglan, (Caernarfon), for instance- are prominently indicated in gothic script on recent editions of OS maps, but have actually been filled in! Other wells have been left to choke in mud, weeds and rubbish, and the scant remains of any associated building or structure have disappeared. Nature soon reclaims the unfrequented path, and it is sometimes necessary to visit sites in the spring and winter months when the encroaching vegetation is low. Many wells earmarked for inclusion in this gazetteer had to be rejected because they could no longer be found. It is essential to record these wells, and any structures associated with them, for posterity, before they are wholly lost.

The story is not all doom and gloom. The wells at Cwm-twrch, Llanfair Caereinion, Llanfyllin, and Mathern, are among several important sites which have been restored in recent years. And at Trellech and Gumfreston, modern-day pilgrims have renewed the old tradition of hanging ribbons on nearby bushes. Even in today's materialistic society, it seems that the ancient beliefs in the mystical properties of water linger on tenaciously.

PLACES TO VISIT

Francis Jones numbered around 1180 holy wells in his book, and the following gazetteer comprises a mere eighty of the most important sites surviving in Wales today. The deciding factors for inclusion have been ease of access, and visible structural remains; a few important or well-known sites (which do not fit into either category) have also been included. They are arranged in five main geographical areas, and are headed under the nearest town or village - for instance, Llanrhaeadr, *Ffynnon Ddyfnog*. This way the inevitable confusion between similarly named wells is avoided. All were visited between 1990 and 1999, and so the descriptions are up-to-date. Current access arrangements are noted at the end of each entry, and grid references are provided for plotting the sites onto the popular OS 'Landranger' series of 1:50,000 scale maps. Place-name spelling is based on current OS maps. I have also provided a rating system to indicate the most outstanding sites worth visiting; it is inevitably subjective, and I apologise in advance if anyone feels their local well has been unfairly treated!

*** Important site, well worth a visit.

** Worth visiting if in the area.

* Only dedicated well hunters need visit. (This category also includes sites not normally accessible to the public, and not visible from any path or road)

SOUTH-WEST WALES

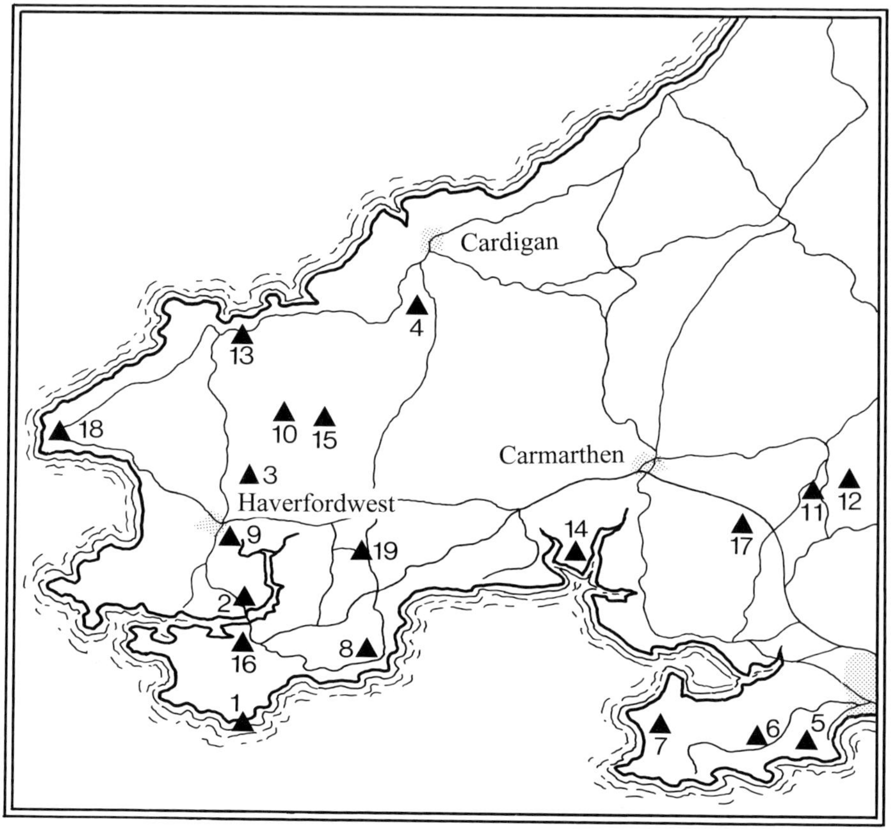

1 Bosherton, St Govan's Well
2 Burton church well
3 Crundale, St Leonard's Well
4 Eglwyswrw, Pistyll Meugan
5-7 The Gower peninsula
 5 St Peter's Well
 6 Ilston Well
 7 St Cenydd's Well
8 Gumfreston church wells
9 Haverfordwest, Higgon's Well
10 Henrys Moat, Bernard's Well
11 Llandybie, Ffynnon Gwenlais
12 Llandyfan, Ffynnon Gwyddfan
13 Llanlawer, Ffynnon Gapan
14 Llansteffan, St Anthony's Well
15 Maenclochog, Ffynnon Deilo
16 Pembroke, St Nicholas' Well
17 Porthyrhyd, Capel Erbach & Capel Begawdin
18 St Davids, St Nons & St Justinians wells
19 Templeton, St Margaret's Well

BOSHERSTON, St Govan's Chapel***

Myth and legend far outweigh any established facts concerning St Govan's Chapel. We only know for certain that the little chapel was built in the Middle Ages, probably sometime between 1300 and 1500. There was a particular fad for hermitages and remote religious cells in the fourteenth century, and St Govan's has one of the finest settings of all, squeezed into a narrow cleft in the rocky cliffs above the sea. The little vaulted building looks like it has grown here of its own accord. The identity of Govan is a mystery, but Gawain of Arthurian legend is a less likely contender than the sixth century Gobhan of Wexford; Pembrokeshire after all, had strong Irish connections in the Dark Ages.

Of the countless folk-tales concerning this sacred site we need only single out one relating to the well itself. The water was used to heal poor eyesight, rheumatism and lameness, and those travellers cured of their ills would leave their crutches and walking sticks behind on the chapel altar. Sadly, the well has been bone-dry for many years, although the roughly built stone canopy can still be seen among the rocks. The chapel is actually built over a small spring, and the water seeps into a small square hole in the floor beside the doorway. Legend has it that the water would never flood the chapel, and devotees would lift out the precious supply with a limpet shell.

Location: Bosherston lies about 7 km south of Pembroke, off the B4319 to Castlemartin. The road to St Govan's is sometimes closed for army training so check in advance. There is a car park on the cliff top with steps leading down to the chapel, but if you want to experience anything of the sacred atmosphere of this site, avoid peak periods! (SR 967 929).

St Govan's Well

BURTON CHURCH WELL**

In total contrast to the wealth of legends enshrouding St Govan's, virtually nothing has survived about the well at Burton church. Neither traditions nor reputed healing properties have been recorded, and even the name of the patron saint of Burton is lost (although the south aisle bears a dedication to St Andrew). Several springs break out of the hill below the church, and the main source fills a rectangular stone bath partly surrounded by flagstone forecourt and retaining wall. The overflow fills an adjoining pond brimming with watercress. Despite some modern renovation work the well looks quite old, but the lack of folklore might suggest it only ever had local significance.

Location: Burton lies on the hillside above the Cleddau river, about 7km east of Milford Haven, off the A477 road to Pembroke Dock. There is a signposted turn to the village as you approach the Cleddau Bridge (SM 985 056).

Burton Church Well

CRUNDALE, St Leonard's Well *

Within the sheltering ramparts of an Iron Age hillfort, the Norman invaders of Pembrokeshire established a foothold in the early twelfth century. There was a castle here, a chapel, holy well and, presumably, a small settlement. As late as 1398 the rector of nearby Rudbaxton parish church was still celebrating mass at *'the chapel of St Leonard beside Simon's Castle'*. All that now remains of this Medieval urban venture is the well, set into the east side of the massive hillfort rampart. A little stone arch was built over it at the beginning of the twentieth century, when the water was considered good for eye problems; now, sadly, the recess is dry and choked with earth and stones.

Location: OS maps show a public footpath leading from the road to the fort, but it is now very overgrown & neglected. The tree-covered site lies next to a minor road 1.5km north-east of Crundale village, off the B4329 from Haverfordwest (SM 985 188).

EGLWYSWRW, Pistyll Meugan*

Only the copious spring remains of this Medieval shrine, in the foothills of the Preseli Mountains. The disappearance of an adjoining chapel is due to the overzealous work of Protestant reformers in the sixteenth century. It seems that pilgrimages had continued to this remote spot after the Dissolution of the Monasteries, but during the reign of Elizabeth the Privy Council decided enough was enough. Three men were instructed to travel *'to the place called St Meugans.... and there to cause to be pulled down and utterlie destroyed all reliques and monuments of that chapell'*. Not one stone was to be left standing, and anyone trying to rebuild the shrine was to be apprehended. Although the buildings were razed, local people still visited the well and fairs were held here on certain days of the year. The spring was believed to contain three distinct waters that never mixed; one was considered good for eyes, one for curing warts and the third for rheumatism and lovesickness.

Location: The spring rises just east of Pistyll Meugan farm, which lies next to the B4332 road to Boncath, 3.5km east of Eglwyswrw (SN 172 379).

THE GOWER PENINSULA **

Beyond the urban sprawl of Swansea stretches the glorious Gower Peninsula, an area rich in archaeological remains and spectacular coastal scenery. The underlying limestone gives rise to numerous springs, and several have been graced with religious connotations, such as St Illtud's well (Llanrhidian and Oxwich), St David's well (Llangyfelach) and Holy well (Reynoldston). Buildings or structures associated with wells are fewer, and there are just three sites which deserve to be included here.

The nearest to Swansea is **St Peter's Well** and chapel near Murton, which takes a bit of tracking down. The easiest way is to follow the signs from Swansea to Mumbles, and then on to Caswell Bay. From the car park at the beach, walk inland along the wooded valley for about 600m, and then take the left-hand fork up the hill. Near the top, in woods to the right, is a group of ruined Medieval buildings. The chapel with its large east window is easy to identify, and just beyond it is a small square building, thought to be a priest's house. A short distance away a little stream rises out of a slab-lined recess in the hillside. When the site was excavated in the 1890's the foundations of a larger structure was revealed, and two hundred years earlier the local historian Isaac Hamon wrote: *'St Peters well is very firm walled and stone benches and pavement belonging to it, it never friezeth, it continueth the stream be the weather wet or dry'*. On the village green at nearby Murton is a charming little well of later date, which does not appear to have any tradition associated with it, but is worth a visit. An old iron pump stands by.

Further along the main coastal road (A4118) at Parkmill, the popular Gower Inn marks the beginning of a footpath along the Ilston valley. After about 400m, a fenced-off ruin will be seen under the trees on the right. This is the remains of **Ilston Chapel**, built in 1649 by the rector John Miles, on, or near, the site of the Medieval Trinity Well. Isaac Hamon suggests that both buildings were still here in the 1690's: *'There is in ye southern part of this parish a well called Trinity Well, by the same there is an old religious house and a chapell'*. The spring still rises at the outer end of the ruin.

On now to the end of the peninsula, where Llangennith village lies clustered around the fourteenth century priory church. On the green is **St Cenydd's well**, which was sealed up in the nineteenth century to prevent animals fouling the supply. The cold water now pours out of a modern spout. Old etchings show that the well was originally surrounded with boulders, and roofed with a large flat stone carved with a cross. Perhaps this was a reused Dark Age memorial stone, or a Medieval grave slab. Cenydd was a local saint who was cast adrift in a basket when a baby, and reared by seagulls on a nearby island. His story is carved into the church gates, and inside can be seen an intricately-carved slab reputed to be his tombstone.

Location: all sites are freely accessible and can be reached from Swansea along the main Gower roads. Caswell via the B4593 (SS 590 884), Ilston via the A4118 (SS 553 895), and Llangennith (SS 428 914) off the B4295 at Llanrhidian.

A modern spout now occupies the site of St Cenydd's Well, Llangennith, Gower

GUMFRESTON CHURCH WELLS ***

The little hamlet of Gumfreston retains an air of tranquillity far removed from the bustling coastal resort of Tenby barely 2km away. From the churchyard gate a path leads down the hillside, past the ruined walls of a priest's house, to the three bubbling wells beside the fourteenth century church of St Lawrence. Rough stone walling embraces two of the springs, and while the structural remains may be less impressive than at certain other holy wells, the serene and peaceful atmosphere makes Gumfreston one of the most evocative places in all Wales.

Gumfreston Church Wells

According to tradition, the uppermost spring is pure water, the middle gives a flow of chalybeate, and the lower one sulphur; but the distinctive taste and red sediment of iron oxide indicates that they are all chalybeate. Bubbles of natural gas frequently break the surface of the mossy pools. The wells were formerly held in great repute for medicinal purposes. By the 1830's plans were drawn up to enclose them and built pump houses and changing rooms for the benefit of visitors from Tenby. Perhaps fortunately this was never carried out. On Easter day local people would visit the wells and drop pins in the water, a practice called 'throwing Lent away'. Very recently another custom has been started here. For a small donation modern visitors can make a wish, or a prayer, and hang a ribbon and bell from one of the trees overhanging the springs.

Location: From the outskirts of Tenby, follow the signs along the B4318 to St Florence. After about 2km you enter Gumfreston village, and a left turn brings you to the church (SN 109 010).

HAVERFORDWEST, Higgons Well***

For many years this Medieval well-chapel was thought to be lost, but then the charming little building was rediscovered in the neglected and overgrown garden of a ruined cottage, and was carefully restored. The plentiful water supply (which is said to never run dry, even in severe droughts) has been tapped for commercial use - the only holy well in Wales to be exploited in this fashion. Bottled water can be bought locally, or sampled on-site from the spring, although the interior of the well building cannot be entered at present because of health regulations. Such bureaucracy never bothered the weary pilgrims who stopped off here on their way to St Davids Cathedral, to wash their tired limbs in the cold waters. The spring rises in a deep pool covered by a little stone building with a vaulted roof, almost identical to the wells at Brecon and Penrhys, except here there are doorways in both end walls. The uppermost led into a small chapel set at right angles to the well, which was added at a later date, but is now very ruined.

Location: On private land 1km south-east of Haverfordwest town centre. As you cross the main roundabout by the railway station, take the left turn to Uzmaston, then the next right, pass under the railway bridge and park in the designated place. Follow the public footpath along the banks of the Cleddau river, until you pass the big house on the left. The well can be seen in the upper garden (SM 962 151).

HENRY'S MOAT, Bernard's Well *

Bernard is the English spelling of St Brynach, an Irish saint more closely associated with the ancient ecclesiastical centre at Nevern, on the other side of the Preseli Mountains. When the antiquarian Richard Fenton passed this way in the early- nineteenth century, he saw *'a redundant spring close to the ruins of an old chapel, having an upright rude stone marked with a cross'*. This is probably the Dark Age gravestone now kept in the parish church. Only a few scattered stones remain of the little chapel, but the marshy spring still rises in a corner of the adjoining field.

Location: From Haverfordwest follow the B4329 for 16km, then take a right turn after passing Tufton village, towards Maenclochog. After 1km a right hand lane leads to Bernard's Well farm. A public footpath passes close to the spring on the west side of the yard (SN 054 280).

LLANDYBIE, Ffynnon Gwenlais **

Llandybie lies on the edge of the Black Mountain, where high rainfall conspires with the underlying limestone to form numerous caves and springs. Commercially available Brecon Carreg Water is bottled nearby, and the river Loughor bursts out of a subterranean labyrinth in one of the most powerful resurgences in Britain. Another copious spring forms the source of the river Gwenlais, which flows out of the ground beside a five hundred year-old yew tree. According to the antiquarian Edward Lhuyd (1660-1709), there used to be a chapel here, and in the early-nineteenth century Richard Fenton recorded a tradition that the water rose when a virgin was murdered. Even the place-name reflects some aspect of this story, for *gwen-lais*, literally translates as the white, or 'pure voiced'. There is no sign of any building here now, just a modern weir forming a deep, cold pond.

Location: The well lies 2km north-west of Llandybie on the A483 between Ammanford and Llandeilo. Just north of the village take the left turn to Milo, and after 1 km there is a wide bend with a small road branching left. Follow this for about 0.5km, and the source of the Gwenlais will be seen in a field on the right (SN 600 161).

LLANDYFAN, Ffynnon Gwyddfan **

Across the valley from Ffynnon Gwenlais the limestone substrata gives birth to another copious spring of pure water. The resurgence beside Llandyfan chapel fills a rectangular nineteenth century stone baptistry, and the flow is so strong that it has to be controlled by a sluice-gate. Richard Fenton visited the 'Welsh Bath'(as it was called) around 1804, and commented on the *'waddyish, unctuous appearance'* of the water. Did he mean the sandy sediment deposited by the stream?

The spring reputedly cured paralysis and numbness, and in the sixteenth century as many as 200 people at a time congregated here. The Protestant authorities made some arrests, but a sympathetic magistrate dismissed the charges, saying that the prisoners were not there on a religious pilgrimage, but were just taking the waters for medicinal purposes. Nonconformists performed the first local baptisms here, and at the end of the nineteenth century the chapel and well were rebuilt and the abundant supply piped to Llandeilo town 5km away.

Location: Llandyfan lies on the mountain road from Trapp to Glanaman, about 5km south-east of Llandeilo. The easiest way is to take the A474 road out of Ammanford towards Pontardawe, then follow the signposted left turn to Drefach & Trapp. You should pass the church on your right after about 5km (SN 642 171).

LLANLLAWER, Ffynnon Gapan ***

A surprisingly large and primitive-looking stone vault covers the wishing well at Llanllawer, in the foothills of the Preseli Mountains. The interior is cool and dark, and the rough walls are encrusted with mosses and liverworts. Only a little stream of water runs out, but the chamber measures 2.9m long and 1.9m high and is large enough for immersion. There are traces of foundations before the entrance, and so perhaps the water was once dammed up behind a retaining wall. The stonework is impossible to date - it could be medieval or fairly modern - and it was restored in the 1980's. A gate now prevents animals from wandering inside.

Ffynnon Gapan, Llanllawer

Richard Fenton recalled a tradition that good wishes were granted by dropping in a pin, but a crooked pin would fulfil evil thoughts. The adjacent church was rebuilt in the nineteenth century, but preserves two cross-stones of 600-800 AD set up on either side of the gate (to prevent evil spirits from entering). And only 1km along the lane to the east is a group of Bronze Age standing stones. Therefore was Llanllawer church established here by the Early Christians to stamp out a lingering tradition of pagan practices?

Location: The well is signposted in a field beside Llanllawer church, which can be reached from Fishguard either along the B4313 to Narberth, or the A487 to Newport (SM 987 360).

Carved Cross on stone beside the gate to Llanllawr Church (Chris Barber)

LLANSTEFFAN, St Anthony's Well **

Unlike Llanllawer's roomy vault, little St Anthony's Well is barely large enough to get your hand inside for a drink of water. But you must wait patiently for the clear drops to seep from the mossy recess in the hillside. By 1811 the existing stonework had been built around the natural spring, in the form of a pointed arch with an 'offerings shelf' at the back. A small recess above the shelf is where a statue of the saint was reputedly placed. In more modern times the surrounding area has been rather heavily improved with extra retaining walls and a paved forecourt. Originally this must have been a very quiet and shady glen, frequented only by lovesick travellers intent on casting a pin into the well to fulfil their heart's desires.

Location: Llansteffan lies 11km south-west from Carmarthen along the B4312. Walk along the path to the ruined castle, then follow the signs around the hillside and down into a wooded valley. The spring is off the path to the right (SN 346 099).

MAENCLOCHOG, *Ffynnon Deilo* **

Only a stony mound in a tree-ringed graveyard remains of St Teilo's church at Llandilo, yet this is one of the oldest Christian sites in Wales. The original church was perhaps founded by St Teilo himself, for two inscribed memorial stones of c.500 AD used to stand guard at the gate. Both have been removed to Maenclochog for safe keeping, and a third stone was taken away to Cenarth. Clearly Llandilo was an important resting place for local dignitaries in the Dark Ages.

Just east of the adjoining farm house is a little brick pump-house on the site of Ffynnon Deilo. The curative properties of the spring were renowned, and the water was used to treat chest complaints such as whooping cough and tuberculosis. Even in 1917 people dropped pins into the well to 'wish' a speedy end to the Great War. For the healing powers to work, the water was drunk early in the morning out of Penglog Teilo, a cup-like fragment of a skull reputed to be a relic of the saint.

The survival of this pre-Reformation relic is surprising enough, but the story of its perambulation around the world is even more remarkable. St Teilo was buried at Llandaff, near Cardiff, and his shrine was damaged in the Owain Glyndwr uprising of the early fifteenth century. A local magnate, Sir David Matthew, carried out repairs to the tomb and was rewarded with hereditary guardianship of a silver reliquary containing the skull. It is thought that the last of the elder line died at Llandilo in 1658, and the relic passed to the local Melchior family. For many years the skull was used in the well-ritual and was filled and handed to the pilgrim by the senior member of the family. In 1927 it was sold for £50 to a descendant of Sir David's brother, whose heirs had settled first in Ireland, then emigrated to Australia. After much detective work the skull was traced to a Sydney bank vault, and in 1994 was at last returned to its original resting place in Llandaff Cathedral.

Location: Llandilo lies 2km east of Maenclochog village on the B4313. Follow a minor road to Llangolman, and take the first turning on the right. The church lies just beyond the large farm on the left (SN 099 269).

PEMBROKE, *St Nicholas' Well***

To get to this well you will have to pass The Old Conduit and walk along Watery Lane; and these place-names give a clue to the history of St Nicholas' Well. This spring was utilised as a water supply for the priory and hamlet of Monkton, which lies just an arrow's shot from the towering battlements of Pembroke castle. The Benedictine priory of St Nicholas and St John was founded in the late-eleventh century and became the parish church at the Reformation. The priors were probably responsible for tapping the source and directing the stream along an open culvert to the stone conduit, which still stands by the roadside opposite the priory.

Restored view of St Nicholas' Well

At the spring, there is a circular stone chamber 1m across with a small entrance and a domed roof. There are signs that the entrance has been narrowed, and the original doorway had 'shouldered' arches characteristic of thirteenth and fourteenth century architecture. Sadly, this interesting little building is now very neglected and practically buried in thorns and brambles. It really should be restored for posterity before its condition deteriorates further.

Location: From Pembroke town follow the signs to Angle (B4320) and on entering Monkton village, turn left along Watery Lane. Walk along this public footpath (very muddy) and follow the stream uphill. After a while the stream leads off into a field on the right, to where a dense clump of bushes hides the well (SM 976 010).

PORTHYRHYD, *Capel Erbach & Capel Begawdin* *

These two ruined buildings are among the more substantial well-chapels remaining in Wales, and yet they are neglected and little-known, and have only recently appeared on OS maps. Capel Begawdin lies deep in a swampy wood on private land. It is a simple oblong building, measuring 8.5m by 4.8m internally, with a bell-cote over the west door and an inserted chimney. Evidently it was reused as a dwelling after the Reformation. The interior is a muddy swamp at present, and it is not clear how the water was channelled through the building.

Only 2km away is Capel Erbach, a similar building, but slightly larger, measuring 5m by 11m. It is set into the side of a narrow stream valley, beside the old parish road and a ruined cottage. The side walls are very ruined, but the west gable is virtually intact and has a fine arched door and trefoiled window, suggesting a date around 1300. The spring rises in the far corner next to the altar, passes along a slab-lined drain in the floor, and emerges through a spout beside the entrance. Above the spring is an arched recess that may have held the statue of a saint, though the dedicatee of Capel Erbach is unknown. Sprained or broken limbs were held under the cold stream, and quartz pebbles (presumably votive offerings) have been found in the drain.

Location: Capel Begawdin is located on private land, south of Maes-Achddu farm, off the old A48 Llanddarog to Crosshands road (SN 511 147). For Capel Erbach branch off at the Mansel Arms, and follow the road uphill for 500m. A lane on the right leads down to the chapel. Ask permission to visit it at the new house (SN 529 147).

Capel Erbach

ST DAVIDS CATHEDRAL ***

'And so we came to the end of the world where the patron Saint of Wales sleeps by the western sea ' wrote the diarist Francis Kilvert in 1871. And pilgrims have been visiting the shrine of Dewi Sant for centuries. In fact, during the Middle Ages two pilgrimages to St Davids were considered the equal of one to Rome. Around the cathedral and along the main approach roads, numerous shrine chapels were established to receive the prayers and coins of devout pilgrims. And the income was substantial. As late as 1603, long after the Reformation had dealt a death-blow to such practices, the local historian George Owen could recall how the votive offerings were brought into the cathedral by the dishfull, there to be divided amongst the clergy. The Reformation and subsequent neglect has seen the loss of many sites, and now only traditions and place-name evidence graces natural springs like Ffynnon Llygaid (Clegyr Boia), Ffynnon Faiddog (Whitesands Bay) and Ffynnon Dewi (Porth Clais). Only two of the subordinate chapels survive above ground today, and the best preserved lies 2.5km west of the cathedral, on the cliff-top near the Ramsey lifeboat station. This is **St Justinian's chapel** (SM 724 252), a roofless ruin built in the early sixteenth century by Bishop Barlow, on the site of an older building and Early Christian cemetery. According to legend, St Justinian was murdered on nearby Ramsey Island, but picked up his severed head and walked across the sea to the present site. Such a miracle allowed him to be enrolled among the highest, and his bones were later moved to share the same reliquary as St David. There were also chapels and wells on Ramsey Island, and John of Tynemouth (d1350) wrote that a man with a swollen stomach drank the water to seek a cure. He immediately threw up a frog and got better. St Justinian's well lies directly opposite the chapel, beside the road. The spring is now sealed and protected by a little round stone building. The masonry is probably post-Reformation, and an almost identical well can be seen at Rhosson Farm on the road to the cathedral.

St Non's Chapel (SM 751 243) also has a splendid coastal setting and lies beside a modern Catholic church, just under 1km south of the cathedral. The shattered building is of uncertain age and is not orientated in the usual east-west fashion; tradition alone identifies this ruin as a chapel dedicated to Nonnita, mother of St David. Nevertheless, early graves have been discovered here, and a simple ring-cross of the period 600-800AD was found embedded in the wall. Legend again fleshes out the sparse bones of history, and tells how the violated virgin gave birth here during a terrible thunderstorm, and a spring of pure water burst out of the ground nearby. The curative and magical properties of the waters were invoked well into the eighteenth century, long after the chapel had been ransacked and ignominiously used as a leek garden. There was a Medieval building over the well, with a stone roof and benches around the walls, but this was replaced with the existing structure by the cathedral authorities in the early eighteenth century. The water rises in a stone trough covered with a rugged, rounded vault 1.4m high and about 1.5m deep. In the side wall there is a niche for offerings, but most modern pilgrims drop their coins into the water, adding to the glittering collection at the bottom of the pool.

Location: Freely accessible, although St Justinian's chapel is on private land. The cathedral city of St Davids lies 24km north-west of Haverfordwest, along the A487.

St Non's Well, St Davids (Chris Barber)

TEMPLETON, ***St Margaret's Well*** **

Place-name evidence suggests that the warrior-monks the Knights Templar had some involvement with the development of this village. Even today the Medieval pattern of narrow building plots running back from the main street is well preserved. In a small hollow in thc fields west of the village lies St Margaret's well, which once supplied the inhabitants with water. The little spring still flows, and is enclosed by a protective curve of masonry with a modern slate capstone. In an adjoining field can be seen the overgrown mound of a Norman castle.

Location: Templeton lies 2km south of Narberth on the A478 to Tenby. After passing through the village turn right along the A4115, and beside a garage on the right is a waymarked footpath which crosses the fields to the well (SN 111 116).

St Margaret's Well, Templeton

SOUTH-EAST WALES

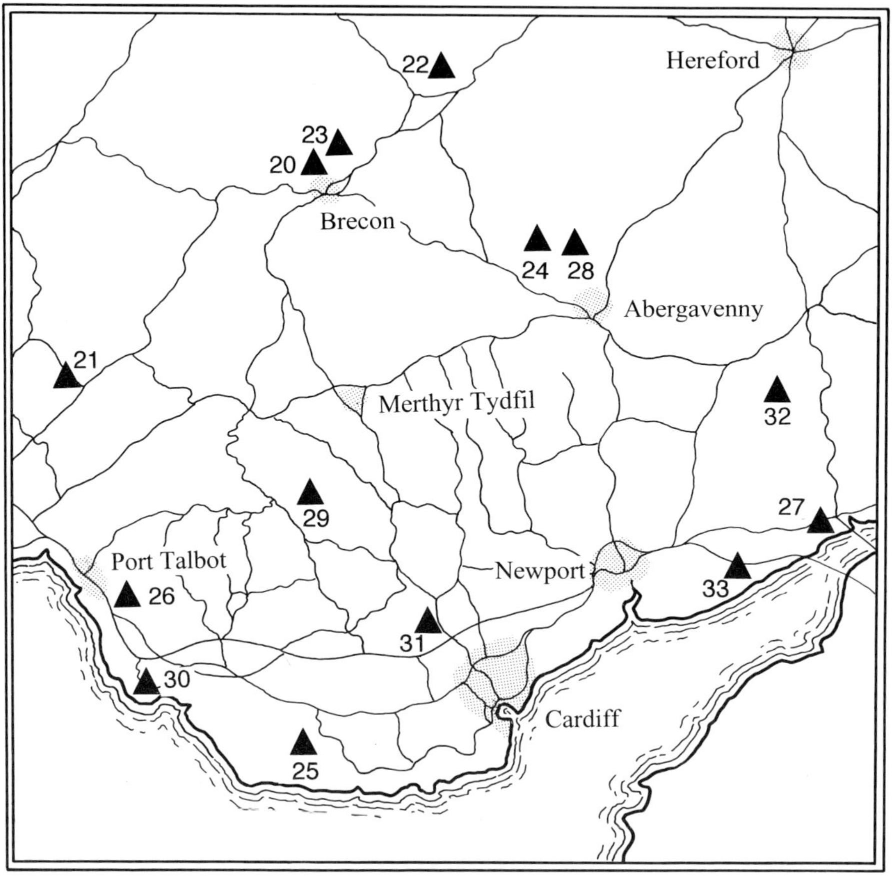

20 Brecon, Maen-du Well
21 Cwm-Twrch-Isaf, Ffynnon Ddrewllyd
22 Glasbury, Ffynnon Gynydd
23 Llandew, Bishop Gower's Well
24 Llangenny, Ffynnon Geneu
25 Llanmihangel, St Anne's Well
26 Margam, Ffynnon Gyffyr
27 Mathern, St Tewdric's Well
28 Patrishow, Ffynnon Ishow
29 Penrhys, St Mary's Well
30 Porthcawl, St David's & St John's Wells
31 Taffs Well
32 Trelleck, The Virtuous Well
33 Wilcrick, The Wishing Well

BRECON, ***Maen-du Well*** ***

This charming little building rarely gets a mention in guidebooks, which is a shame, for it is one of the finest surviving in the country today. Francis Jones made a passing reference to it, and mentioned the tradition that it was a 'wishing well' for lovelorn maids. The vaulted stone building looks quite ancient, and resembles Early Christian chapels and monastic cells still surviving in Scotland and Ireland. However, a stone by the entrance has the initials WW and the date 1754, proving it to have been built (or perhaps rebuilt?) in relatively recent times. The building is small, measuring only 1.7 by 1.5m square, and is roofed over with a high pointed vault formed of overlapping slabs. Beyond the low door with its massive lintel slab is a flight of worn steps, which descends to the bubbling spring. A ring of rough boulders in the bed of the pool could be the remains of an older well-building, predating the eighteenth century structure.

The beehive-shaped chamber over Maen-du Well, near Brecon

Brecon has another site worth tracking down if you are visiting the nearby cathedral. At the far end of the graveyard a lane curves down the hillside to a spout of fresh water pouring out of a stone wall. There is a cobbled forecourt and a retaining wall incorporating some reused Medieval stonework. Like Maen-du, pins were dropped into the water to make a wish come true.

Location: The cathedral lies on the west side of the river Honddu, and is signposted from the town centre. Follow the road uphill past the church, and take the last turn on the left into Maes-y-ffynnon housing estate. Take the first right, and follow the road to a parking area. Maen-du well is in a landscaped enclosure beside the road (SO 038 297).

CWM-TWRCH ISAF, *Ffynnon Ddrewllyd* ***

This spa has experienced a small revival in recent years, and there are even road signs pointing the way to 'Ffynnon Cwm-twrch'. The older name, however, is far more relevant. The 'smelly well' is a natural sulphur spring with a characteristic stink of rotten eggs discernible at twenty paces. The Victorians were assured that such high mineral content and olfactory delights were good for the health, and flocked here to drink and wash in the water; even bottling the stuff for future use. The annual Cwm-twrch Eisteddfod was held here, and the riverside meadow beside the well was a popular meeting place and recreational area on Sundays. The well was restored in 1920 and again in 1993. All the stonework is modern and forms a cul-de-sac leading into the steep hillside, the water pours out into a concrete bowl heavily encrusted with sediment. Donít forget to hold your nose when taking a drink!

Location: The village lies on the A4068 road from Ystalyfera to Brynamman in the upper Swansea valley. Turn left past the Post Office, walk over a bridge, and the well will be found behind a row of houses (SN 764 104)

GLASBURY, *Ffynnon Gynydd* **

What looks like a roadside bus shelter is, in fact, a timber-framed canopy built around 1900 to enclose and protect St Cynidr's well. It was set up in memory of Walter de Winton of nearby Maesllwch Castle, killed in action in Africa in 1892. Beneath the trapdoor in the floor is a pool of clear water enclosed by four large slabs, with a circular inlet hole cut in one side. How old is this simple structure? A *Fynon Kynid* is mentioned in 1653, but the RCAHMW suggested in 1913 that the original well may have lain behind a demolished cottage on the other side of the road. Another spring rises in the enclosed overgrown area behind the well, and this could repay careful excavation at a future date. The Medieval church is some distance away in the Wye valley, and so this remote hamlet at the meeting point of several roads could be the site of the original Early Christian settlement.

Location: Fynnon Gynydd lies in the hills off the A438 between Glasbury and Llowes, near Hay-on-Wye. Follow the signposted road to Maesyronen (one of the oldest Nonconformist chapels in Wales), for 2.5km to the village. The well is by the roadside (SO 164 413).

Ffynnon Gynydd, Glasbury

Bishop Gower's Well, Llanddew (Chris Barber)

LLANDDEW, ***Bishop Gower's Well*** **

The little village of Llanddew is dominated by the austere thirteenth century church and the ruined walls of a fortified palace owned by the Bishops of St Davids. Beneath a great stone arch in the crumbling outer wall is a square pit filled with a dark pool of water. The entrance is now covered with a grill, but the villagers used to get their supply from an iron pump standing nearby. The well is named after Bishop Henry de Gower (d.1347), an enthusiastic builder who also constructed lavish palaces at the cathedral city and Lamphey in west Wales.

Location: By the roadside opposite the church. Llanddew lies about 2km north-east of Brecon, and is signposted off the B4602 (SO 054 308).

LLANMIHANGEL, ***St Anne's Well*** *

The gaze of anyone passing through the little village of Llanmihangel is bound to be drawn to the rambling sixteenth century mansion of the Thomas family, or the slightly less prominent church of St Michael. Most inconspicuous of all is St Anne's Well, now barely visible in a densely overgrown enclosure beside the churchyard gate. The murky spring rises in a small rectangular stone pool, and drains away into a marshy stream. Originally the water entered the pool through the breasts of a eroded human figure, carved onto an upright slab. This has been missing for a long time, but fortunately a drawing of it was published in *Archaeologia Cambrensis* 1888. Judging from the print, the 'breasts' were crudely drilled holes in what may have been a reused Medieval grave slab.

Location: The village lies about 3km south-west of Cowbridge in the Vale of Glamorgan. Best reached along the B4270 to Llantwit Major, then follow the signs through Sigingstone to Llanmihangel (SS 982 719).

MARGAM, ***Ffynnon Gyffyr*** ***

The Cistercian abbey of Margam fell victim to Henry VIII in 1536, and only a few fragments of the Medieval building remains, overlooked by the gaunt hilltop ruin of Hen Eglwys. At the foot of the hill below the chapel OS maps mark the site of Ffynnon Pedr, but this is rather hard to find and the feeble spring is surrounded on three sides by low crumbling stonework. However, in nearby Cwm Maelwg is a far more impressive holy well that has not only been omitted from modern maps, but received just a passing reference by Francis Jones. This is a substantial little stone building with a vaulted roof, which is partly built into the steep hillside and measures 2m by 5.6m. Within the cold and echoing chamber steps lead down into a stone-lined bath in the floor, which is fed by a constant supply of water from a spout in the end wall. The bath would have been filled to a depth of at least 1.2m, but the water now seeps out through the ruined stonework and emerges lower down the hill. Presumably the well is late-Medieval in origin, but the finer quality of the stonework around the bath suggests it may be a later alteration. This splendid building is in a rather poor state of repair, and deserves to be restored for posterity.

Location: From M4 junction 38 follow the signs to Margam church & museum, and after a sharp right bend, take the lane forks. Take the left branch, which leads to a small car park beside the lake. From here walk uphill along the road for 500m and take the next right turn down through the forestry to the well (SS 803 869). For Ffynnon Pedr, at the fork walk west along the rough track for about 500m. The spring is not easy to find, it lies a few metres from the path on the left hand side, in a dense clump of rhododendrons (SS 795 865).

Ffynnon Gyffyr, Margam

MATHERN, ***St Tewdric's well*** **

Despite the gloss of tradition, Tewdric, or Theoderic, was not a true saint, but a Christian warlord engaged in stemming the flow of Saxon invaders in the Dark Ages. Some researchers even believe he was the grandfather of the 'real' King Arthur. According to the twelfth century *Book of Llandaf*, Tewdric abdicated in favour of his son Meurig, and retired to live in the solitude of the Wye valley. However, an angel inspired him to fight the pagans once more and, joining forces with his son, he won a decisive victory at Tintern in 470. But he was mortally wounded in the conflict, and asked to be buried (in true Arthurian fashion) on an island in the Severn sea. Tewdric was taken from the battlefield on a sled dragged by two stags as far as the banks of the estuary, where the makeshift carriage broke apart and a spring burst out of the ground. There he died, and Meurig built an oratory over his grave which in time became the large and grand Medieval church of Mathern. The place-name derives from the Welsh *merthyr teyrn*, or martyred king.

St Tewdric's well lies by the road just north of the church, and is marked with a commemorative plaque set up by the local council in 1977. The well was unsympathetically restored at the time, with a harsh concrete enclosure wall and steps leading down to a deep, mossy pool.

St Tewdric's Well, Mathern (Chris Barber)

There is a slight chalybeate taste to the water. The stonework covering the spring itself is much older though, and the low chamfered arch could be late-Medieval. Perhaps more likely it was built in the early-seventeenth century by the Bishop of St Davids, who restored the grave of Tewdric and placed a memorial plaque on the walls of the chancel.

Location: Mathern is about 2.5km south-west of Chepstow off the A48 to Newport. Just west of Pwllmeyric village take the signposted left turn and continue beyond the motorway flyover. The well is fenced off on the right (ST 523 912).

Unsympathetic restoration of St Tewdric's Well by local council (Chris Barber)

PATRISHOW, ***Ffynnon Ishow*** ***

The little shrine of Patrishow lies in a fold of the Black Mountains, an area long used as a retreat for the contemplative pilgrim. St Ishow established his cell here in the Dark Ages, then Augustinian monks founded a priory at Llanthony in the early twelfth century. Eight hundred years later Father Ignatius started a modern monastery at Capel-y-ffin. Patrishow has outlasted them all. According to legend the waters only became curative after the unfortunate saint was murdered by a traveller and dumped in the well (the place-name is a corruption of the Welsh *merthyr* [martyr] *Ishow*). In the early eleventh century a weary pilgrim from the continent, ravaged by the dreaded leprosy, washed away his ailment, and gratefully gave a hat-full of gold to enable the first church to be built here.

Patrishow Church lies on the hillside above Ffynnon Ishow

The inconspicuous well lies on the riverbank below the church, and consists of a square stone-lined recess set into the steep bank, covered over with a flat slab. Offerings used to be placed in a niche in the back wall, but at the time of my visit it was filled with a little cross made from twisted grass. The winter rains had filled up the pool, but at other times of the year the supply is less. *'A very scanty oozing of water'* noted the antiquarian Richard Fenton, *'to which was formerly attributed great virtue'*.

However, the real treasure of Patrishow is the Medieval church, clinging precariously to the steep sides of the Gwyrne valley. The oddly-placed chapel at the west end is likely to mark the site of St Ishow's cell. Inside the main building there is an intricately carved wooden rood-loft which miraculously survived destruction at the Reformation, and a series of wall-paintings including a skeletal 'doom' figure armed with a spade and hourglass.

Location: Patrishow lies about 10 km north of Abergavenny off the A465 Hereford road. Turn off at Llanfihangel Crucorney & follow the B4423 to Llanthony for 2km. Take a left turn and follow the signs all the way to the church (SO 277 224).

Ffynnon Ishow (Chris Barber)

PENRHYS, ***St Mary's Well*** ***

Modern day Penrhys is a sprawling council estate on a bleak mountain-top above the Rhondda Valley, but five centuries ago it was one of the most visited places in Wales. In the Middle Ages the Cistercian Abbey of Llantarnam in Monmouthshire acquired a large tract of upland territory, and probably established a grange (farm) here. What began as a humble sheep farm soon grew into a lucrative and important pilgrimage centre, drawing people from all over the country. Surviving poems praise the shrine of St Mary and the virtues of the healing well; *'There are rippling waters at the top of the rock. Farewell to every ailment that desires them. White wine runs in the rill, that can kill pain and fatigue'* wrote one bard. Within the chapel stood a wooden effigy of St Mary which was believed to have fallen from Heaven, and had miraculous healing powers. But the dark years of the Reformation brought to an end the monastic glories of Penrhys. Bishop Latimer wrote to the king's ministers claiming that the statue was *'the Devyll's instrument to brynge many (I feere) to eternal fyre'*, and to prevent local unrest the shrine was pillaged at night. The statue was taken to London and burned, and Penrhys crumbled into obscurity.

St Mary's Well, Penrys is situated high above the Rhondda Valley

Today only a fragment of the chapel remains above ground, but the spring still flows within an attractive little stone building on the hillside. The masonry could be late-Medieval in origin, but has been restored several times. A low door leads into the single chamber, which measures just under 3 by 2m, and is roofed with overlapping slabs. There is a square cistern in the floor, fed by a piped source of water, and an offerings niche in the upper wall. The water was used for baptisms in the parish church, and was considered good for rheumatism, scrofula and sore eyes. Penrhys was reinstated as a Catholic shrine in 1947 when 4000 people made a pilgrimage to the well.

Location: Penrhys estate lies on the B4542 Ystrad to Ferndale road in the Rhondda Valley. From the bus stop on the summit, a footpath leads down the hillside to the well, which overlooks Llwynypia (ST 001 945).

Statue of the Virgin Mary at Penrhys (Chris Barber)

PORTHCAWL ***

The twin hamlets of Newton and Nottage have almost been swallowed up in the expanding coastal resort of Porthcawl, yet three holy wells have managed to survive on the fringes of this urban development. Oldest of all is **St David's well** at Nottage, which gave its name to the little valley of '*Dewiscumbe*' mentioned in twelfth century documents. There was a chapel here as well. This has now disappeared and the spring nearly suffered the same fate; by 1935 all that could be seen was 'a muddy heap of stones by the way-side'. It is not certain how much of the present structure is the result of subsequent restoration. Certainly the square forecourt is modern, but the semi-circular well pit, roofed over with large rough slabs, looks much older and could be Medieval.

About a quarter of a mile away in the shadow of a new road and roundabout embankment, is **Ffynnon Fawr**. The murky spring is encased in a modern stone building with an arched entrance and forecourt, but if you peer into the low vaulted tunnel you will see a smaller, rougher arch, which could be part of an older structure. A plaque on one side of the well has a didactic verse in English and Welsh extolling visitors to remember the divine provider of all good things on earth: '*Cofiwn Awdur pob daioni / Wrth yfed dwr o'r ffynnon fawr*'.

Ffynnon Fawr, Porthcawl

Another poem graces the rugged stone walls of **St John's Well** at Nottage, further east. This was written by Sir John Stradling of St Donatís Castle, and appeared in an edition of Camden's *Britannica* published in 1610. Sir John recalled the belief that the waters ebbed and flowed with the tide, and likened this event to a 'battle' between the nymph of the Severn, and the guardian spirit of the well: '*As the Nymph doth rise, the spring doth fall, / Go she back, he com's on, in spite and fight continuall*'. Originally this was known as Sandford's Well, presumably after the De Sanford family who held lands here in the Middle Ages. There was a circular enclosure nearby where bonfires were lit on Midsummer eve to drive evil spirits away. The head of the well is covered by a modern vaulted building which has been extended on one side in a vain attempt to disguise an electrical sub-station. Beyond the locked door a narrow passageway and flight of stone steps descends a surprisingly long way into the ground, ending at a dark, mysterious pool.

Location: St David's well (SS 821 786) lies north of Nottage village beside a minor road to Moor Lane; while Ffynnon Fawr (SS 822 781) is below the roundabout on the B4283 Porthcawl to Corneli road. Newton (SS 836 773) is east of Porthcawl, just off the A4106 Bridgend road. The well is on the village green below the church.

St John's Well at Nottage (Chris Barber)

Taffs Well in 1861

TAFFS WELL ***

According to local tradition, people have been visiting the warm springs at Taffs Well for centuries, and 'Roman' stonework was supposedly discovered in 1799 when a flood washed part of the ground away. However, it was only in the later nineteeth century that the success of this little spa really took off. There were several springs here on the banks of the river Taff, and one source was enclosed in a little metal shack. This crude structure is depicted in an etching published in Hall's *Guide to South Wales* (1861). There was only room for two or three people inside, and the well could have been nothing more elaborate than a water-filled pit in the ground. The guide mentions that the springs were *'tepid, and have a slight mineral tinge'*, and were considered very effective for rheumatism and lameness. People queued at all hours to bathe, women leaving a bonnet hanging on the door, and men their trousers, so that newcomers would know the gender in occupation! The farmer charged an entry fee, but was reluctant to provide better facilities or exploit the adjacent springs. A subsequent owner raised a cottage-like building on the river bank around 1890, but by 1929 the heyday of the Welsh spa was over, and the spring was in a poor state of repair.

Local people set about revitalising the spa and added an open-air swimming pool supplied by warm water from the spring. The pool was still in use in the late 1950's, but repeated flooding from the river soon brought the life of the spa to an end. The little building was almost buried in a flood embankment, and suffered much vandalism and neglect, before it was again restored and given a facelift of rusticated stone.

There is no public access at present, but through the barred doorway you can see a small brick chamber filled with cloudy water. The warmth is caused by surface water percolating so far underground that it is heated by natural thermal energy, before being forced back up to the surface. Although it is not as hot as the famous spring at Bath, on a cold day you can see the steam rising from the water.

Location: The modern well building lies beside the bowling green in the middle of the town, on the A4054 north-west of Cardiff, M4 junction 32(ST 120 836).

The modern construction enclosing Taffs Well (Chris Barber)

PENLLYN, SALMON'S WELL ***

This is one of the very few and fortunate examples of a holy well rescued from neglect and decay by the efforts of a local community. In 2000 the three wells at Penllyn village were cleared of debris and undergrowth, the masonry restored, new fences, footpaths and information plaques provided, all carried out as a Millenium Project. However, this is not the first time that the wells have been preserved for public benefit. At the end of the nineteenth century Dr Salmon of Penllyn Court footed the bill for necessary repair work, and since then the springs were named in his honour.

One of three wells at Penllyn

Finds from recent excavations include coins, pottery fragments, and clay pipes of eighteenth and nineteenth century date, but it is likely that the springs had been in use long before then.

Most of the masonry that can now be seen must date to Dr Salmon's time, but it is possible that the two wells nearest the road are pre-Reformation in origin, and there is an offerings niche in the back wall of one. Both are covered by modern-looking stone buildings with gated doorways, but the actual spring inside is protected by older and rougher masonry. For centuries this was the only reliable source of water for the parish in drought, and around 1911 a third well was dug at the head of the dell. But with the advent of piped water, visits to the well slowly petered out, and the whole site fell into neglect in the 1930s.

Location: The three wells lie in a fenced enclosure beside the road just north of Penllyn Village, off the A48 about 2.5km west of Cowbridge in the Vale of Glamorgan (SS 973767).

Author's Note: Information on the restoration of this site came to light too late for it to be included on the map.

TRELLECH, *The Virtuous Well* ***

The Virtuous Well, or St Anne's Well, is the most substantial holy well remaining in the old county of Monmouthshire. Francis Jones lists some 65 sites, but the majority are just springs without any protective masonry. There is said to have been nine wells at Trellech originally, but since there is a nearby hamlet called Ninewells, the story may have arisen due to confusion over the place-name. The spring rises in a small round chamber with a domed roof, set into a stone wall, and originally protected with a little wooden door. In front of this is a semi-circular paved forecourt, surrounded by stone walls and a low bench.

The 'virtues' of the well were renowned in the seventeenth century, and the antiquarian Edward Lhuyd (1660-1709) noted that the water was '*very medicinall to such as have the scurvy, collick and other distempers*'. Although said to have been a strong chalybeate spring, the characteristic taste of iron is not readily detectable today, and it may be that modern restoration work has affected the quality and level of the water supply. A drawing published in Sir Joseph Bradney's *History of Monmouthshire* (1913) shows the well overgrown with weeds and the surrounding ground almost level with the top of the wall, so that the forecourt was effectively a sunken bathing pool.

The Virtuous Well, Trellech

Aside from the medicinal quality of the spring, it was also widely used for making wishes; a pebble was dropped into the water, and if a lot of bubbles appeared the wish would be granted immediately, if only a few bubbles arose, there would be a delay, and if none at all, -then better luck next time! A large number of rags fluttering from the overhanging hawthorn bushes testifies that the Virtuous Well is still a popular pilgrimage site. It is also one of the 'three wonders' of Trellech, the others being an impressive group of Bronze Age megaliths, known as *Harold's Stones*, and *Tump Terret*, the grassy mound of a Norman castle. All three are commemorated on a fine sundial (now inside the parish church) erected in 1689 by the wealthy Probert family of Pant Glas. On the panel depicting the well is a Latin inscription which reads *'Magdalen Probert gives proof of it'* - presumably a reference to the efficacy of the water. The fine quality of the stonework suggests that the existing well-house was built at this time by Lady Magdalen. There is another spring with a modern stone canopy, at the road junction just south of the village.

Location: Trellech lies on the B4293 Chepstow to Monmouth road. If approaching from Monmouth, follow the signposted road for about 7km, then pass through the village (Tump Terret is beyond the church). At the triple junction, take the left turn to the well, which lies in a field a short distance along on the left (for Harold's Stones take the right turn) SO 503 051.

The old sun dial in Trellech Church drawn by Fred Hando

WILCRICK, *The Wishing Well* **

Virtually nothing is known or recorded about the history of this holy well, and even the meticulous Francis Jones missed it. A spring of cold, clear water rises in a circular stone basin, which is roofed over with a brick and stone dome. The use of brick suggests that the existing structure is unlikely to be earlier than c1800, but since the hamlet of Wilcrick nestles at the foot of a large Iron Age hillfort, it is tempting to think that the well has a very early origin. Presumably it was dedicated (like the adjacent church) to St Mary, and would have been used as a water source by the inhabitants of the Medieval manor.

Location: On the village green at Wilcrick, just off the B4245 to Newport, 1km west of M4 junction 23a (ST 409 880).

The Wishing Well of Wilcrick

MID WALES

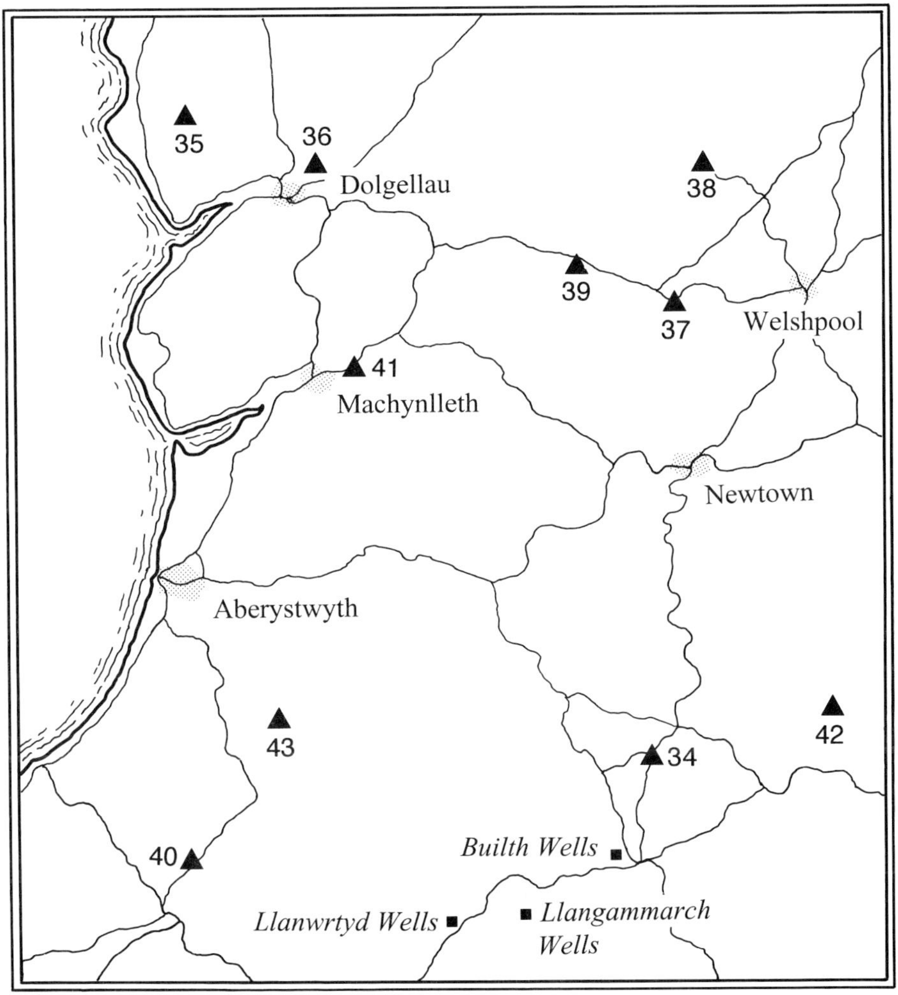

34 Llandrindod Wells
35 Llanenddwyn, Ffynnon Enddwyn
36 Llanfachreth, Ffynnon y Capel
37 Llanfair Caereinion, St Mary's Well
38 Llanfyllyn, St Myllyn's Well
39 Llangadfan, Ffynnon Cadfan
40 Llangybi, Ffynnon Gybi
41 Penegroes Well
42 Pilleth, St Mary's Well
43 Swyddffynnon, St Ffraid's Well

LLANDRINDOD WELLS***

Only at Llandrindod can you sample the rich mineral water that brought fame and fortune to the spa towns of mid Wales. Among the arboreal walks in Rock Park below the town is a marble spout set into the hillside, out of which dribbles a flow of chalybeate so rich in iron as to be barely drinkable. No wonder Dr Linden considered that the medicinal waters *'give place to none in Europe'* (1756). The history of the spa has been outlined in the introduction; here it is only necessary to describe the buildings which have survived to the present day. Beside the Arlais brook is a chequer-work brick building with an adjoining glazed pagoda-like conservatory, dating from 1908-9. Here the health seeking visitors would congregate during the summer months to imbibe the water. Saline water at breakfast, sulphur in the mornings and afternoons, and a glass of chalybeate as an aperitif with meals. Trade declined in the early twentieth century as more and more people opted for the seaside holiday, and in the 1972 the spa finally closed. However, the departed glories have been recently revived; the buildings were restored in the 1980's (they now house a tea room and alternate medicine centre), and every year in August the shops are decked out and local residents dress up in period costumes to celebrate the town's Victorian heritage.

Location: Llandrindod Wells lies on the A483 between Builth Wells and Newtown in mid Wales. The spring and spa buildings can be found in Rock Park off Norton Terrace (SO 055 610).

LLANENDDWYN, *Ffynnon Enddwyn* ***

Try to pick a fine day to visit this site, for it lies high in the mountains overlooking Tremadoc Bay and the sweeping arm of the Lleyn peninsula. At over 700m above sea level, this is arguably the most spectacularly located holy well in Wales.

According to legend St Enddwyn was cured of an illness after bathing here, and subsequent pilgrims would leave their crutches behind if they too, were blessed with good health. The water was drunk to cure scrofula, and moss from the well was applied as a plaster or poultice. The extremely remote location is unusual (the parish church is over 4km away), and this suggests that Ffynnon Enddwyn is either a genuinely early site, or one that was considered to be particularly efficacious and worthy of a long trek. The cold, clear water rises in a little rounded basin and overflows into a square bathing pool about 2m across. The whole structure is roughly built from the lichen-spotted boulders that lie strewn across the mountainside. In 1921 the RCAHMW suggested that the bath may have been built in the eighteenth century, but there is no real way to date this site; the crude rubble walls could have been standing for a hundred years, or even a thousand.

Location: From the village of Dyffryn Ardudwy (A496), follow the signs uphill to Cwm Nantcol. The road is steep and narrow, and you will have to pass through two gates. The well lies a short distance downhill from the road, through a signposted gate in the wall. There is a parking place a short distance beyond the gate (SH 614 255).

LLANFACHRETH, *Ffynnon y Capel* *

The name of this site suggests a Medieval chapel stood nearby, but no trace remains today, and the well itself may not be long for this world. In 1833 Samuel Lewis described it as a *'spring of excellent water'*, but it is now fenced off, very overgrown, and hidden beneath metal sheets. The roadside spring rises in a pool about 6m square, and the visible stonework looks fairly modern.

Location: Llanfachreth lies in the mountains 6km north-east of Dolgellau, and can best be reached by following the signposted road north out of the town centre, and turning right once over the flyover. At the village take the sharp left turn, and the well is in the field on the left hand side of the road, just before a farm track (SH 751 224).

LLANFAIR CAEREINION, ***St Mary's Well*** **

From the grandly Victorianised church of St Mary a path winds through the graveyard to a shady ledge beside the river Banwy, where the parish holy well can be found. A flight of stone steps leads down into a large rectangular bath filled with rather dirty water to a depth of two feet. This was clearly meant for bodily immersion, but the water was also used as a charm against curses and witchcraft. The spring fell into disuse and neglect for many years, until the crumbling stonework was restored in 1990.

Location: Below the church in Llanfair Caereinion village, which lies about 12km west of Welshpool along the A458 (SJ 104 065)

LLANFYLLIN, ***St Myllin's Well*** ***

Fifteen centuries ago the Breton St Moyling (Myllin in Welsh) is said to have baptised his followers at this well.The clear water trickles out of a mossy spout at the back of an arched stone recess, set into the steep hillside above the town. In 1987 the well was restored and the surroundings transformed into an ornamental garden with rockeries and ponds.

St Myllin's Well, Llanfyllin

According to Francis Jones, Ffynnon Myllin was one of ten sites in Wales where sick pilgrims would tie rags to branches in the hope of a cure. On Trinity Sunday local people would gather here to drink the water sweetened with sugar, before retiring to the local inn for a feast of cakes and ale.

Location: Llanfyllin lies on the A490 about 15km north-west of Welshpool. Signposts in the town point the way up Coed-y-llan hill to the well, which is best reached on foot (SJ 138 195)

LLANGADFAN, ***Ffynnon Gadfan*** **

Buried in a hedge-bank beside a country lane is a low, dark stone-lined passage leading down to a pool of clear water. This is St Cadfan's well, and we are very fortunate to be able to visit it at all. In the nineteenth century the well was about to be destroyed for road building, but the local rector intervened and so the embankment was built over it instead. Much of the surviving structure must date from that time, but there was an older and more substantial building here before. In his *Topographical Dictionary of Wales* (1833), Samuel Lewis wrote that Ffynnon Gadfan was *'anciently covered with some building* [constructed from] *stones of remarkably large size*'. He also added that the well was *'formerly in great repute for the marvellous efficacy attributed to its water*'. A faded plaque beside the road outlines the history of the sixth-century saint and his healing well.

Location: Llangadfan lies on the A458 10km north-west of Llanfair Caereinion. As you approach the village take the left turn by the big hotel, cross the bridge and turn sharp right. A few metres along the road there is a small gate in the hedge on the right hand side leading to some bungalows. The well is beside this path (SJ 012 104).

LLANGYBI, ***Ffynnon Gybi*** ***

Not to be confused with the better-known well on the Lleyn peninsula, this Llangybi lies in the Teifi valley, and was voted best kept village in 1990. Ffynnon Gybi is well kept too; a signpost points the way to the strong, clean spring of pure water flowing from under a stone slab in the corner of a field. According to the antiquarian Edward Lhuyd this was also known as Ffynnon Wen, and was frequently visited for a kill-or-cure treatment for scrofula, scurvy and rheumatism. *'On Ascension Eve they resort to Fynnon Wen; after they have washed ymselves at ye well They go to Lhech Gibi... There they put ye sick under ye Lhech*' If the patient managed to sleep, then they would recover; if not, then death would follow. From another manuscript version of Lhuyd's text, it is clear that the 'llech' was a large slab supported on smaller stones, which sounds very much like a Neolithic burial chamber, or cromlech, although one no longer survives here today.

Location: the village lies 5km north-east of Lampeter on the A485 to Tregaron. The well is in the field opposite Maesyffynnon chapel (SN 605 528).

PENEGROES WELL**

Every year until his death in 1904 the local rector tended the roadside well at Penegroes village. The subsequent state of inevitable neglect was reversed in 1980 when the stone pools were cleaned out but, alas, twenty years on and the site is unkempt and overgrown again. This sad state of affairs was not always so; people suffering from rheumatism came here in great numbers to bathe in the cold water. In Samuel Lewis' day the roof had gone and the rectangular pool (effectively divided into two baths by the central steps) was open to the sky. As for the age of the building, the surviving stonework does not look very old, and this may be an eighteenth century spa rather than a true holy well.

Location: In a field beside, and slightly below the A489, opposite the old school house in Penegroes village, 2km east of Machynlleth (SH 768 009).

PILLETH, *St Mary's Well* **

Pilleth church is a lonely, little-frequented building, revelling in peaceful isolation on the hillside above the Lugg valley. But the scars of a tempestuous past are all too evident here. In the fields nearby can be seen the earthworks of a Norman castle, one of many in this disputed border region, and in 1402 the forces of Owain Glyndwr inflicted a bloody defeat on the English here, and burnt the church down. It was rebuilt, only to fall victim to another conflagration in 1894, and remained a gutted shell until repairs were carried out in 1910. In the Middle Ages the church contained a miraculous wooden effigy of St Mary, 'Our Lady of Pilleth' which, along with the healing well, drew pilgrims to this remote and verdant valley. The statue has long gone but the well is still here, and can be found in a shady corner behind the church, next to the ruined tower brought down by Glyndwr. Six steps descend into an oblong, stone-lined pool, which is currently in a poor state of repair and held in place by wooden props. During recent clearance work some stone tiles were found, suggesting that it may have been roofed over.

Location: Pilleth lies about 6km south-west of Knighton, off the B4355 to Presteign. Follow the road signs all the way to the village, and the church will be seen high on the hillside. It is reached by a grassy track past Pilleth Court Farm (SO 256 683).

SWYDDFFYNNON, ***St Ffraid's Well*****

The spring that gives this little village its name still flows into a hollow beside the main road, but the well dedicated to the Irish St Bride (Ffraid in Welsh) lies 1.5km away in the back garden of Gwenhafdre Farm. St Ffraid is one of the oddest of Welsh saints. She sailed across from Ireland in the sixth century on a chunk of turf, and was held in considerable respect by the Early Christians. Her CV of miracles range from the respectable (turning inanimate objects into food for the poor) to the ridiculous (letting her eyes fall out to deter a would-be lover, then popping them back in when he had gone).

Over the spring is a roughly built drystone building very similar in appearance to Maen-du at Brecon, but far too small to allow any access. The water rises in a dark and mossy circular pool within the chamber and flows into a modern cistern outside. This attractive little well is undateable; the simple structure could be early, and it has been linked to the Welsh Cistercian abbey of Strata Florida on the opposite side of the valley. Did the monks use the well as a refreshment stop on their travels? There are no traditions associated with it, and during recent clearance and restoration work only finds of post-Medieval date were recovered from the chamber.

Location: On Gwenhadfre Farm - ask permission at the house to visit. Swyddffynnon lies 2km south-west of Ystradmeurig Village, on the B4340 Tregaron to Aberystwyth road. Pass through Swyddffynnon (the village well is on the right in the dip), then take the first right turn. The second right turn then leads down to the farm (SN 674 670).

St Ffraid's Well, Swyddffynnon

NORTH-EAST WALES

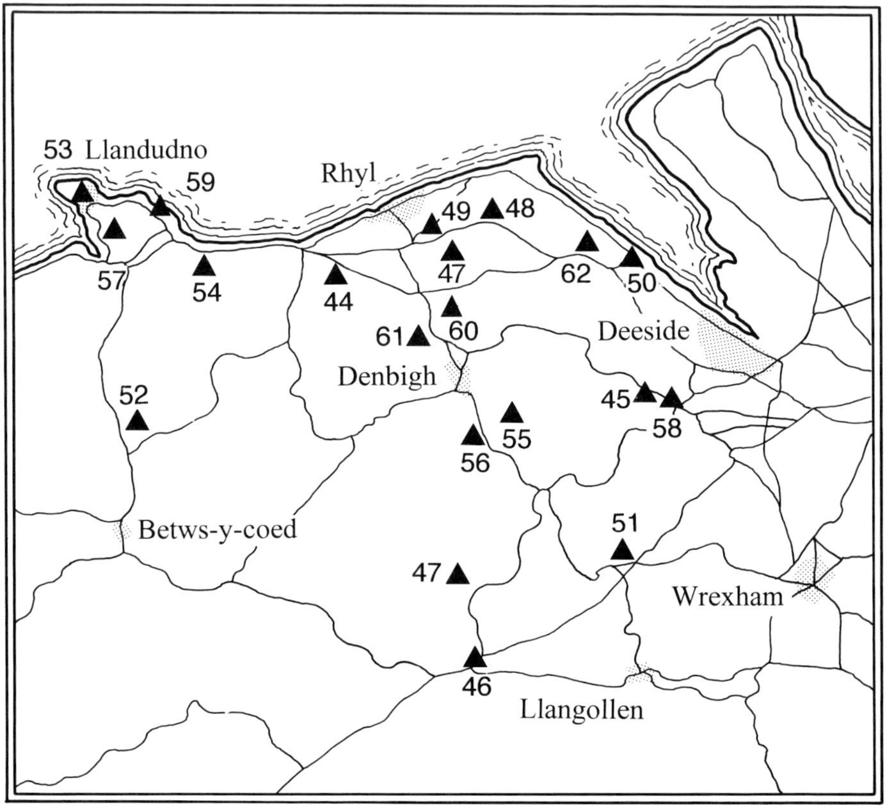

44 Abergele, St George's Well
45 Cilcain, Ffynnon Leinw
46 Corwen, Ffynnon Sulien
47 Derwen, Ffynnon Sarah
48 Dyserth, Ffynnon Asa
49 Gwaunysgor, Ffynnon Wen
50 Holywell, St Winefride's Well
51 Llandegla, Ffynnnon Tecla
52 Llanddoged, Ffynnon Ddoged
53 Llandudno, St Tudno's Well
54 Llanelian-yn-Rhos, Ffynnon Elian
55 Llangynhafal, St Cynhafal's Well
56 Llanrhaeadr, Ffynnon Ddyfnog
57 Llanrhos Well
58 Mold, Rhual baptistry
59 Rhos-on-Sea, Capel Trillo
60 Tremeirchion, Ffynnon Beuno
61 Trefnant, Ffynnon Fair
62 Whitford, St Oswald's Well

ABERGELE, ***St George's Well****

In the immaculately kept landscaped grounds of Kinmel Hall, is a fenced-off enclosure engulfed in conifers and scraggy undergrowth. This inauspicious site is one of the strangest wells in Wales, for the only 'pilgrims' ever to benefit from its healing waters were horses! Sick animals were brought here, sprinkled with water, and the blessing *'Rhad Duw a Sant Sior arnat'* uttered (The grace of God and St George upon you). Money was then placed in the church poor box. According to Edward Lhuyd, this was known as a horse well from at least the seventeenth century. Francis Jones noted a similar tradition performed on the saint's day in Russia.

Beneath the jungle of weeds the well building appears to be mostly intact, and consists of a rectangular enclosure large enough to accommodate three horses at a trot. In the floor of the chamber are two pools of different sizes, and the varying quality of the rough stonework suggests that the existing structure could be an enlargement of an older, and smaller, building. Local people cleared the site in the 1970's, but it has recently become very overgrown again. Only restoration and a detailed survey would help unravel the origins of this curious site.

Location: The well lies just within the entrance to Kinmel Park and permission is required to visit it. However, it can just be seen from the gate, at the eastern end of St George village, 3km south-east of Abergele off the A547 (SH 976 756).

CILCAIN, ***Ffynnon Leinw*** ***

When inspectors from the RCAHMW visited this site in 1910, they observed that the well had dried up (except after rain), possibly as a result of quarrying nearby; but in the intervening years the water has returned and Ffynnon Leinw is full to the brim. Rough stone walls enclose a sunken rectangular pool 6m by 3m which was clearly intended for immersion. According to the traveller and writer Thomas Pennant (1781) there was an outer enclosure wall surrounding the pool, but only a few tumbled stones remain of this. A few years later Samuel Lewis described Ffynnon Leinw as *'a copious and limpid spring... much resorted to for bathing'*. Edward Lhuyd also knew about this spring, and it is quite possible that the crumbling stonework is Medieval. According to legend the water is supposed to rise and fall with the sea, and so perhaps the tide was out when the inspectors visited it!

Location: The well lies 7km west of Mold beside the A541 to Denbigh. After passing the Royal Oak pub, there is a small marshy wood on the left, and the well can be found among the trees at the further end (SJ 186 677).

CORWEN, *Ffynnon Sulien* **

Corwen has an unusually large graveyard and documentary evidence of carved stone monuments, suggests that this church in the vale of Dee was a particularly important religious centre in the Dark Ages. According to Edward Lhuyd there was a well nearby called *Ffynnon y gloch felen*, which was named after the discovery of old bronze bell (possibly a handbell of Celtic type). The church is dedicated to the sixth century missionary, St Sulien of Britanny, whose name is usually linked with his compatriot St Mael. Water drawn from St Sulien's well was used for baptisms in the church, and since the two sites are over 1km apart and separated by the swift flowing Dee, then the spring must have been considered very important to necessitate the long trek. In 1564 the spring was known as *Fynnawn Silian*. The well still gives a strong supply of water and rises in the garden of a small cottage. Stone steps lead steeply down into a hollow where massive flagstones enclose the duckweed-covered spring.

Location: The well in on private land, but ask permission at the cottage to visit. From Corwen take the A5 toward Bangor for 2km then take the right turn to Ruthin (A494). After you pass the turn for Rug Chapel, there is a lay-by on the right & a lane leading down to the well (SJ 068 441).

Ffynnon Sulien, Corwen

DERWEN, ***Ffynnon Sarah******

Sheltered by a grove of conifers and holly bushes on the banks of the Mynian brook, Ffynnon Sarah's idyllic setting is only marred by a stern sign warning that the water is 'not suitable to drink'. But why not? For hundreds of years the well was reputed to offer cures for cancer and rheumatism, and those healed would discard their crutches at a nearby cottage. The cottage burned down in 1860 and the site fell into neglect, until the rector tidied up the grounds in the 1970's. Despite the name, the well is actually dedicated to the Irish saint Saeran, and the bubbling water rises in a rectangular stone enclosure measuring 4.5m by 2.3m. Four stone steps lead down into the 1m deep pool, where patients would immerse themselves, before throwing in a pin for good luck.

Location: Follow the signs from the A494 Corwen to Ruthin road to Derwen. Pass through the village, and take the sharp right turn to Clawdd-newydd. After about 0.5km, a grove of trees on the left marks the entrance to the well (SJ 064 515).

Ffynnon Sarah, Derwen

DYSERTH, *Ffynnon Asa***

The Medieval chronicler and cleric, Gerald of Wales (1146-1223), mentioned a wonderful well near Rhuddlan which ebbed and flowed with the tide. He may very well have been writing about Ffynnon Asa, which bursts out of the foothills of the Clwydian range, and was also credited with tidal properties. However, this tradition was disproved as long ago as the seventeenth century, when a correspondent of Edward Lhuyd watched the unchanging volume of water for nine hours! The well was so popular for medicinal cures (and as a natural spectacle in itself) that many visitors to north Wales stopped by. Dr Johnson was here in 1774, and a few years later the traveller Thomas Pennant wrote that *'the fountain is enclosed with stone in a polygonal form'* (1781). This was perhaps the work of the landowner, who had also deliberately antiquated the site by setting *'neat pillars'* around it. However, an intriguing possibility is that Pennant was actually describing a star-shaped basin like the ones still surviving at Holywell and Trefnant. Unfortunately the well is now covered by a modern reservoir and the copious source (some five million gallons a day) is utilised by the Water Board. There is nevertheless a pleasant walk along the banks of the crystal clear stream, passing the ruins of several old water mills.

On the far side of the mountain stands the village of Cwm, where a small well jointly dedicated to St Mael and St Sulien can be seen in the vicarage wall. It is now dry, and the stone trough lies within a square recess bordering the road. A little further along OS maps mark a 'Ffynnon Cil-haul', which is also mentioned by Francis Jones. It lies at the end of a rocky trench and has a locked metal door - but this is almost certainly an old mine level! Therefore its name and any traditions associated with it must be of very dubious age and provenance.

Location: The village of Cwm lies 2km south-east of Dyserth, and is signposted off a minor road to Rhuallt (SJ 066 774). For Ffynnon Asa, leave Dyserth towards Holywell along the A5151 for about 1.5km. There is a right hand turn along a narrow lane towards Henfryn Hall. At a sharp bend in the bottom of the wooded valley, leave your car, and follow the public footpath upstream to the ruined mill and reservoir (SJ 075 790).

GWAUNYSGOR, *Ffynnon Wen* **

On a hillside below the great Bronze Age burial mound of Gop Cairn is a much less obvious religious site. Water still flows out of Ffynnon Wen, but much of the surrounding masonry is in a poor state of repair, and excavation would be needed to determine what exactly lies buried here. According to the RCAHMW much damage was caused around 1910 by the reckless landowner, who was *'incensed by the number of visitors to the well'*. A photograph published in the Flintshire Inventory seems to show the remains of a vaulted building. Today the crumbling foundations remain of two small buildings, set at right angles to each other. One of them may have been a small chapel, a changing room, or even a caretaker's cottage. The other is the well itself, a stone lined pool 1.7m wide and at least 3m long. Although the name means 'white well' in Welsh, the earlier spelling of '*Ffynnon Wynne*' might suggest it was associated with the Wynne family of the nearby manor. Edward Lhuyd knew it as Ffynnon Gwaunysgor. One of the stones beside the spring (just visible in the drawing) is a re-used carved slab which originally formed part of a late-Medieval fireplace.

Location: The well lies next to a public footpath 2.5km south of Prestatyn, and can be reached from the A5151 Rhuddlan to Holywell road. About 2km east of Dyserth there is a signposted left turn to Gwaunysgor. Follow this until you reach a sub station opposite Bryn View house. The signposted footpath starts on the right hand side, and climbs uphill across an open field, passing the well in a fenced-off copse (SJ 082 803).

The ruins of Ffynnon Wen, Gwaunysgor

HOLYWELL, ***St Winefride's Well*** ***

The grandest and most famous of all Welsh holy wells, St Winefride's well has a tradition of virtually uninterrupted pilgrimage from the Middle Ages to the present day. In addition, this magnificent Perpendicular building has managed to survive almost unscathed, seemingly in defiance of the vicissitudes of religious worship in Britain. According to tradition the shrine originated in the seventh century, when a young maiden, Winefride (Gwenfrewi in Welsh), was pursued by a lusty local prince. When she persistently refused his advances, he angrily drew his sword and cut off her head. Where the head fell, a great spring burst out of the ground. Fortunately, her uncle St Beuno emerged from a nearby church, placed her head back on her shoulders, and restored her to life. Winefride later joined a convent at Gwytherin, and rose to become abbess before her (final) death. However, her grave was such a popular attraction for pilgrims, that the monks of Shrewsbury (desirous for lucrative relics) moved her bones to their abbey in 1138.

The legendary origin of the well clearly mixes fact and fiction, as well as Christian and pagan Celtic imagery. No doubt the huge resurgence at the head of the Greenfield valley had been an object of wonder for centuries, but the earliest reference to a pilgrimage here is in 1115, when the site was owned by St Werburgh's Abbey at Chester. From 1240 to 1537 the chapel and healing well came under the control of nearby Basingwerk Abbey and, despite occasional damage sustained during the long Anglo-Welsh wars, the shrine flourished, and the countless pilgrims included the high and mighty. *'The king [Henry V] with great reverence, went on foot in pilgrimage from Shrewsbury to St Winifred's Well in North Wales'* (1416); Edward IV and James II also paid a visit. The money collected from the shrine was substantial, and a lot must have lined the pockets of the clergy. In 1480 the Abbot of Basingwerk had *'twice the treasure of a king in wine'*!

Whatever Medieval building stood here did not survive a radical reconstruction around 1500, under the patronage of Lady Margaret Beaufort, mother of Henry VII. An elaborate two-storied building was constructed, with a chapel at upper ground level, and a crypt over the spring itself. The basic plan of the building is a rectangle, with an imposing buttressed facade pierced with three large arches. Inside the dark and echoing crypt, the powerful spring rises in a star-shaped basin, topped with a lattice-work of slender stone pillars and arches. Pilgrims would immerse themselves in a sunken bath approached at either end by stone steps. Over all is a complex vaulted roof enriched with a riot of carved decorations, culminating in a pendant boss over the well depicting events from the life of St Winefride. Numerous carvings also grace the exterior of the building,

St Winifred's Well, Holywell

Cutaway reconstruction of Holywell showing the upper chapel and vaulted crypt with the elaborate star-shaped well chamber including the Tudor emblems of a portcullis and rose, biblical beasts, and three conjoined heads - no doubt a symbol of the Trinity, yet executed in such a primitive style that it recalls the head carvings of the pagan Celts.

Only a few generations after this remarkable building was completed, the Reformation began to transform religious life, and the profitable shrine passed into royal control. From then on the story is one of sporadic attempts to stamp out persistent Catholic pilgrimages and worship at the well. It was a forlorn task. The shrine was one of the most important in Britain, and there are numerous accounts of clandestine (and quite brazen) meetings taking place; '*public Mass is said continually*' moaned the Bishop of Bangor in 1625. Spies were everywhere, innkeepers were encouraged to inform on strangers, yet the faithful still flocked to the well. In 1723 the chapel was converted into a school, and the depredations carried out to the building have only recently been reversed.

In the more tolerant nineteenth century, Roman Catholics regained possession of the well, and bathing cubicles were fitted up for greater privacy. Celia Fiennes had noted in 1698 how the indifferent bathers were '*exposed to all*' while in 1774 Dr Johnson complained about the bath being '*completely and indecently open*'. Thomas Pennant witnessed many pilgrims '*in water in deep devotion up to their chins for hours, sending up their prayers*'(1781). It must have been an ordeal. The traditional ritual was to pass through the bath three times, and then kneel to prey on St Beuno's stone in the stream. The recusant priest John Gerard braved the icy water on a frosty November morning in 1593; '*for a quarter of an hour I lay down in the water and prayed. When I came out my shirt was dripping, but I kept it on and pulled my clothes over it and was none the worse for my bathe*'. Despite all efforts to end worship at the shrine, the nearest it ever came to closure was in 1917, when mining at Halkyn accidentally diverted the underground stream, causing the well to dry up. This catastrophe was only reversed when a nearby spring was tapped, although the force of water pouring out of the well is much less than it used to be.

Not many people know that a second holy well exists here, though it is now difficult to find and is hardly as impressive as its near neighbour. Hidden in the bushes on the hilltop west of the shrine is a marshy spring dedicated to Winefride's uncle and saviour, St Beuno. His name is also linked to a rough boulder in the modern pool adjoining the shrine, where he is said to have stood to pray and deliver sermons.

Location: This famous shrine lies on the hills overlooking the Dee estuary between Flint and Prestatyn, and is well signposted from the town centre (access via the A55, A5026, or A548). The well is cared for by the Catholic Church and there is a small admission charge (SJ 185 763). There is no public access to St Beuno's well (SJ 184 762).

Statue of St Winifride, Holywell (Chris Barber)

LLANDEGLA, ***Ffynnon Tecla*****

This well had a widespread reputation for curing epilepsy, or *clwyf tecla*, a serious illness that required a particularly convoluted treatment, involving the pagan ritual of a 'scapegoat'. According to Edward Lhuyd (who knew someone who had been healed in this fashion), the patient had to visit the well after sunset on a Friday, wash their hands and feet, then walk around the spring three times reciting the Lord's Prayer. All the while the patient had to carry a cockerel in a basket (or a hen, if the sufferer was female). After praying, the bird was pricked with a pin, and the pin was dropped into the water. The prayers and perambulations were repeated three times around the church, then the patient donated some money to the clerk, and slept the night away under the communion table, using the Bible as a pillow. At daybreak the patient would breath into the bird's beak (thus 'transferring' the illness), leave more money, and depart for home. If he heard from the clerk that the bird had died, then it was taken as a sign that the illness had been successfully passed on; if not, then the whole laborious process had to be repeated. In 1749 the Dean attempted to stop these semi-pagan rituals, but the practice continued into more enlightened times; as late as 1850 chickens could be seen strutting around the church.

For such an important and well documented site, Ffynnon Tecla is a bit of a disappointment. In woods on the banks of the river Alun, one of several marshy springs has been enclosed on three sides by low stonework, forming a small pool about 1.5m across. The overflow water trickles away through the roots of two trees growing from the open side. When Thomas Pennant visited Llandegla around 1781 he saw a stone inscribed with the letters AG and EG - presumably the initials of the builders. Perhaps there was a more substantial well-building here then.

In 1935 A D Rees carried out an excavation at the pool, and the results of the dig were published in the *Bulletin of the Board of Celtic Studies* in that year. Under the flagstone floor he found a thin layer of mud containing pins, coins, and pieces of late-eighteenth to early-nineteenth century pottery. Beneath this level was an older layer containing pieces of quartz and calcite, presumably thrown in as votive offerings in the days before metal pins became widely available.

Location: Llandegla village lies just off the A525 Ruthin to Wrexham road. Opposite the church a public footpath leads past a farmhouse dated 1736, and crosses an open field. The well is in the woods immediately to the right (SJ 194 523).

LLANELIAN-YN-RHOS, *Ffynnon Elian*

Although Ffynnon Elian no longer exists, its dreadful reputation as a 'cursing well' renders it a permanent place in the folklore hall of fame. The spring bubbled out of the hillside north of Llanelian village overlooking Colwyn Bay, and until the eighteenth century had a good reputation as a traditional healing well. But by the end of the century things had changed, and increasing numbers of people began to visit the well to inflict bad luck, financial ruin, illness and even death, on those who had crossed them in the walks of life. There was a catch of course; only the guardian who lived in an adjacent cottage could inflict the curse (for a fee), and only the guardian could remove it again (for an even higher fee). In 1820 it cost 5 shillings to lay a curse, and the unfortunate victim had to pay 15 to lift it! One year the custodian earned the relatively huge sum of £300. The psychological effect on the minds of the superstitious was appalling. There is the story of a man who spent his adult life confined to his own farmstead, for fear of dying should he step beyond his property and fulfil a curse laid on him by an enemy. Many other tales and traditions are recorded by Francis Jones.

The most notorious guardian of the well was John Evans, known locally as Jac Ffynnon Elian, who was brought before the authorities for fraud in 1823 and 1831. While serving a six month jail sentence he became a devout Christian and subsequently published a book on the hurtful practices going on. Various attempts were made by magistrates and brave locals to end the vindictive business carried out by the guardians. The well was blocked up in 1829 and 1864, but the water broke out further down the hill and the new sources were utilised instead. By the 1870's however, the heyday was over, and visits gradually petered out. Nevertheless, the memory still lingered on for years.

Location: The well lay on the hillside north of Llanelian church, signposted off the B5383 from Old Colwyn to Betws-yn-Rhos (SH 864 765).

LLANDDOGED, *Ffynnon Ddoged* *

According to Edward Lhuyd there were over forty wells in this parish, and the most important was Ffynnon Ddoged close to the church. It is still here but, alas, the rural setting has been usurped by modern houses, and the greensward has given way to concrete. Beside the entrance to one house is a low, box-like building constructed from flat slate slabs, with a locked wooden door which hides a copious supply of pure water.

Location: The village lies about 2km north of Llanrwst in the Conwy valley, and is signposted off the A470. Take the narrow lane past the church, and the well will be seen on the right beside a modern close named after the ancient spring (SH 805 638).

LLANDUDNO, ***St Tudno's well*****

The rocky headland of the Great Orme bears many relics of the Prehistoric and Medieval periods. There is St Tudno's church, the ruined bishop's palace, a Neolithic burial chamber, and an underground Bronze Age mine complex. The OS map marks several wells on the limestone escarpment, but only two find a place here. On the steep hillside just 90m south-east of the church is **St Tudno's well**, now in a wretched state and barely visible through the undergrowth. A modern brick trough collects water seeping from an older stone-lined cavity in the hillside behind. More accessible is **Ffynnon Rhufeinig** ('Roman Well'), alongside a waymarked footpath 420m west of the church. Now only a dirty pool of water collects in a trough, and all the surviving stonework is modern, but older foundations can be seen behind the wall. The Roman origin suggested by the name seems to be wishful thinking.

Location: The Great Orme is accessible by several roads and paths from Llandudno. St Tudno's well is on private land, but just visible from a sharp bend in the road beside the church (SH 771 838). Further up the hill a trackway leads west below the summit, passing the cable car station. Ffynnon Rhufeinig is in the wall on the left side of the path (SH 766 838).

LLANGYNHAFAL, ***Ffynnon Gynhafal*** **

This well had a widespread reputation for curing warts, but this tradition must have been introduced at a late date, for the size of the chamber shows that Ffynnon Gynhafal was no mere wart-well, but was intended for bodily immersion. The well chamber measures almost 3m across by 5m long and is approached by stone steps, leading down to a deep pool. A crumbling brick vault once completely encased the pool, so that it was, effectively, an underground chamber. This vault was probably built in the nineteenth century, but the lower walls are roughly constructed from local limestone blocks, and are likely to be much older, suggesting that Ffynnon Gynhafal was originally an open pool terraced into the hillside. It was to this much simpler well that the bard Gruffudd ap Ieuan (d.1520) paid a visit to seek St Cynhafal's aid in healing his injured leg.

Location: Llangynhafal lies in the vale of Clwyd about 6km north of Ruthin. The well itself is in the garden of Plas Dolben farm, about 0.5km north of the village crossroads. Permission to visit it must be sought from the house (SJ 133 637).

LLANRHAEDR, ***Ffynnon Ddyfnog*** ***

Llanrhaeadr is one of the finest churches in the Vale of Clwyd, and its great treasure is the kaleidoscopic Jesse window in the chancel. This exquisite piece of late-Medieval art shows the family tree of Jesus and was set in place in 1533, on the eve of the Reformation. It is still here today because someone wisely buried the panes for safe-keeping during the Commonwealth period. Hundreds of pilgrims visited the nearby healing well of St Dyfnog in the Middle Ages, and it was their financial offerings that paid for the glass. According to tradition the spring was imbued with healing powers only after the saint stood in the cold stream as a penance. The Royal Antiquary, John Leland, travelled through Wales in the 1530's and saw *'fonnon Dunnoc... a mighty spring'*. It is indeed a copious stream, issuing in several springs out of a rock outcrop at the head of a little valley, and tumbling down past the church. Edward Lhuyd considered that the water was good for healing scabs, sores and skin complaints; *'and some say twould cure ye pox'*. So popular was Llanrhaeadr in the eighteenth century that changing rooms were added, and Thomas Pennant wrote that the spring was *'enclosed in an angular wall, decorated with small human figures'* with a bathing pool in front. All was in ruins by the early-nineteenth century, and today only the foundation walls of the deep oblong pool remains.

Location: St Dyfnog's church lies 4km south-east of Denbigh on the A525 to Ruthin. A footpath from the churchyard can be followed uphill though the woods to the well (SJ 080 633).

Ffynnon Ddyfnog, Llanrhaedr (Chris Barber)

MOLD, *Rhual baptistry* *

Unlike the other sites mentioned in this gazeetter, this is not a true holy well, since it was built around 1685 by the Baptists of Hill Cliffe in Wrexham, for the sole purpose of baptising new members of the faith. Nevertheless it is structurally identical to many wells around the country (particularly the above-mentioned Llanrhaeadr) and, thanks to restoration work in 1931 and 1991, is in an exceptionally good state of preservation. It lies within the landscaped grounds of Rhual, the seventeenth century ancestral home of the Edwards family, and consists of a well-built oval enclosure, with a central oblong pool 2.2m by 3.7m, and up to 1.4m deep. There were formerly high stone walls ensuring some degree of privacy for the converts, who were immersed in the deep pool filled with crystal-clear water from a copious spring. At a later date a little round changing room was added on one side.

There once existed another important holy well nearby, but this unfortunately fell victim to roadworks in the last century. The Goblin's Well was reputedly haunted, and stood in a field close to the Alleluia Monument. This stone pinnacle can be seen next to the Denbigh road 500m away, and was set up in 1736 to commemorate a victorious Christian battle in the Dark Ages.

Location: On private land, but just visible from the roadside. From Mold town centre take the A541 to Denbigh, and turn left down a narrow road after you pass an industrial estate on the right. Stop by the second sharp bend, and look across the field to your right, and you will see the stone well beside some trees (SJ 227 648).

RHOS-ON-SEA, ***Capel Trillo*** ***

Experts have argued for years over the date of this tiny well-chapel, huddled against the winter storms on the edge of sea. Opinions of age vary from the sixth, to the sixteenth century, and the author of the recent Clwyd edition of *The Buildings of Wales* (1986) saw *'no reason why it should not be early'*. It closely resembles the wells at Margam and Brecon, but no-one would claim them to be Dark Age; perhaps on balance a medieval date is more likely.

Capel Trillo is a simple, plain building constructed from the rounded beach pebbles to hand, with a vaulted roof and slit windows filled with modern stained glass. The narrow door leads into a single low chamber, which measures just 2m by 3m, and in the floor beneath the altar is a square pit where the spring water collects. During restoration work in the late-nineteenth century the original high pointed roof was replaced with a much lower one, and huge buttresses were added to prop up the crumbling walls. In years gone by, fishermen would visit the chapel before sailing to fill their water barrels, and to pray for a good catch. Whenever it was built, Capel Trillo would have occupied a lonely setting on a bleak coastal plain, with only a few scattered farms for company; but over the last hundred years or so, the expanding resort of Colwyn Bay has swallowed up the green fields.

Location: The chapel is only open on Friday at 8am for Holy Communion. At other times the exterior can be freely viewed, and it lies below the promenade (close to the public conveniences) between Rhos-on-Sea and Penrhyn Bay (SH 842 812).

Capel Trillo, Rhos-on-Sea (Chris Barber)

RHUDDLAN, ***St Mary's Well*** ***

Between Rhuddlan and Dyserth stands Bodrhyddan Hall, ancestral home of the Conwy family since the early-fifteenth century. Part of their medieval residence may lie embedded within the grand mansion that now survives here, a relic of extensive rebuilding in the late-seventeenth and nineteenth centuries. The holy well itself lies in a shady grove close to the house, and it is supposed to be an ancient pre-Christian site, but the surviving building is dated 1612. Probably the builder was John Conwy (d.1647) and he is reputed to have employed the famous Jacobean architect, Inigo Jones. Few traditions or curative myths appear to have survived, and it is not certain if this was a typical holy well for the use of travellers and local people, or just an ornamental feature of a private garden. The water rises in a charming little octagonal building and flows into an adjoining oblong bathing pool. The chamber is covered by a pointed stone roof with a carved pelican on the top. The emblem of the 'pelican in her piety' forms part of the heraldic crest of the Conwy family, and its use on a healing spring is particularly apt; in medieval times it was believed that a pelican would give its life-blood to feed its starving young.

Location: the well is in the grounds of Bodrhyddan Hall, which is only open to the public on Tuesday & Thursday afternoons, between June & September. It lies just east of Rhuddlan on the A5151 (SJ 044 787).

TREMEIRCHION, ***Ffynnon Beuno*** ***

Perhaps nowhere else in Wales is the ancient Celtic head cult so obviously connected with a Christian holy well, than at Ffynnon Beuno. The pure spring water pours out of the mouth of a grotesque stone head, fixed into the lower wall of a rectangular bathing pool. Evidently, drinking water was taken from the spout, while pilgrims suffering from rheumatism and other diseases would immerse themselves in the deep, mossy pool. The seventh century St Beuno is associated with this area of north Wales, and was responsible for magically reattaching the severed head of his niece, Winefride, at Holywell not far away. Does the round face with its goggle eyes and gaping mouth spewing life-giving water, meant to represent St Beuno or his headless relative? The origin of the carved stone is unknown, but it does not look like a piece of Dark Age sculpture. More likely it is a reused fragment (perhaps a gargoyle or waterspout) from the nearby parish church, which also contains some notable Medieval monuments.

Location: The well lies in the front garden of Ffynnon Beuno House just south of the village, and can be seen from the roadside. Tremeirchion is in the Vale of Clwyd between Ruallt and Bodfari off the A55 (SJ 084 724).

The healing waters of Ffynnon Beuno at Tremeirchion
pour out of the mouth of a grotesque stone head

TREFNANT, Ffynnon Fair ***

'The ivy that mantles its walls with incredible thickness of leaves - the spring flowers and the green turf, the sparkling waters bubbling along their pebbly course - the never ceasing songs of the woodland choristers... all these compensate, in the mind of the contemplative pilgrim, for the damage so ruthlessly and so needlessly done, and even make the place more lovely than could all the trickeries of sculptured stone, and painted roof and storied glass.'

The Reverend H. Jones' florid praise for the shattered shrine of St Mary, was published in 1847, when early tourists were drawn to the romantic landscape of Wales. The sense of loss evoked by his words is still evident today, for this was one of the finest well-chapels in Wales, a building almost as large and grand as Holywell, but now reduced to stony foundations and crumbling walls. In the centre of this weedy desolation a copious spring still bubbles out of a star-shaped well chamber, and flows in a marshy rill to join the river Elwy.

The star-shaped well basin of Ffynnon Fair at Trefnant, lies within the ruins of Capel Fair

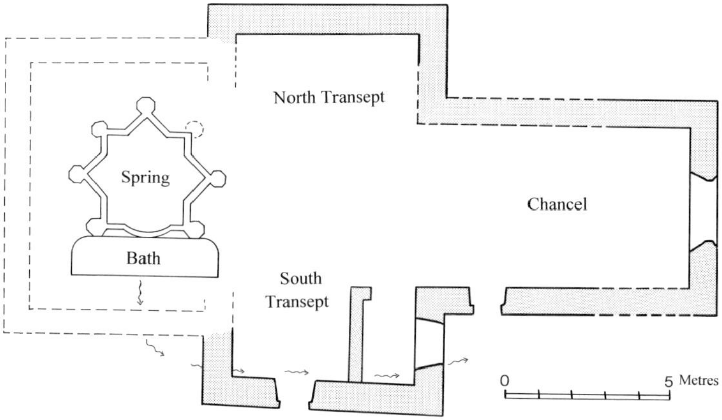

Trefnant, Ffynnon Fair (Plan and conjectural Reconstruction of the well-chapel)

The surviving architectural details suggest that the building was largely constructed around c1500, and was modelled on the more elaborate shrine at Holywell. Ffynnon Fair was never as successful as its rival (the rather remote setting may have weighed against its popularity), and it barely outlasted the Reformation. The records of St Asaph Cathedral refer to surreptitious marriages taking place here as late as 1640, and the roof timbers were still intact in the early years of the eighteenth century. Thereafter the story is one of decay, reversed only in the nineteenth century when the owners tidied up the ruins as an ornamental garden feature.

Ffynnon Fair consists of a long rectangular chapel with transepts on the east and west sides. The well basin actually lies outside the building at the north end, but this part of the site is very ruined and has suffered some alterations in recent times. The finely dressed stonework of the star-shaped bath indicates that there was some form of elaborate vaulting over the spring, probably contained within a projecting wing, and so the building originally had a cruciform plan. The water flows out of the basin and along a channel in the south transept, before meandering down to the river. A recent examination of the site by CADW-Welsh Historic Monuments has indicated that the transepts may be the remains of an older and simpler chapel of oblong plan, which was radically altered by the addition of the chancel and well-basin. Excavation is really needed to unravel the full plan and origin of this fascinating building.

Location: Ffynnon Fair is actually on private land, but a public footpath passes close by. It lies 4km south-west of St Asaph off the A525. Travel south towards Denbigh and on the outskirts of Trefnant take the right hand fork (B5381), and continue down into the valley and over the river. Take the next left turn to Wigfair, and after 0.5km a signposted path on the left leads down past some houses and along the riverbank to the ruined chapel (SJ 029 710).

WHITFORD, *Oswald's Well**

Oswald was a seventh century king of Northumberland, killed in battle against the pagan ruler of Mercia. His principal holy well remains at Oswestry (the traditional site of his martyrdom), but not far from Holywell is another spring bearing his name. A strong spring of water rises in a modern brick chamber, sealed by a rusty iron door, and set into the hillside below an old tree stump. It is on private land, but can easily be seen from the roadside (undergrowth permitting).

Location: 2km west of Holywell along the A5026, turn right onto Mertyn lane and take the next right turn. After 300m along this lane you pass a house on the left side, and the well is in a swampy copse just below the house (SJ 168 777).

NORTH-WEST WALES

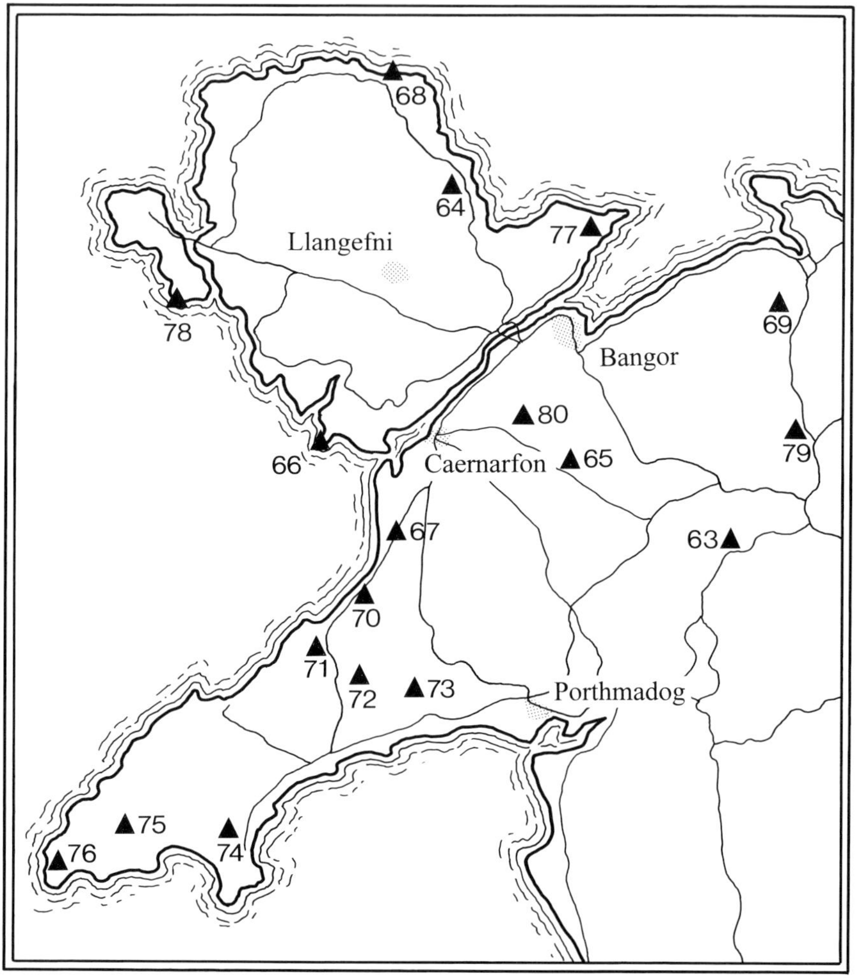

63 Dolwyddelan, Ffynnon Elan
64 Llanallgo, Ffynnon Allgo
65 Llanberis, Ffynnon Beris
66 Llanddwyn Island
67 Llandwrog, Ffynnon Edliw
68 Llaneilian, Ffynnon Eilian
69 Llangelynin, Ffynnon Gelynin
70 Ffynnon Beuno
71 Ffynnon Aelhearn
72 Ffynnon Grasi
73 Ffynnon Gybi
74 Ffynnon Fyw
75 Ffynnon Fair
76 Ffynnon Fair
77 Penmon, St Seiriol's Well
78 Rhoscolyn, St Gwenfaen's Well
79 Trefriw spa
80 Waun, Ffynnon Cegin Arthur

DOLWYDDELAN, *Ffynnon Elan* **

From a crag high above the Lledi valley, the keep of Prince Llywelyn's castle frowns down on the little village of Dolwyddelan. Most visitors stop at the fortress, but how many now visit the little healing well of Ffynnon Elan? It may be as old as the castle, and Richard Fenton (rather optimistically) thought the Romans used it. The water is said to steam in frosty weather, and was considered good for healing paralysed limbs and sickly children. When inspectors from the RCAHMW came here in the 1950's they reported that the well was dry, but it has started flowing again, and gives a plentiful supply of cold mountain water. The spring rises in a crumbling stone basin about 2.7m square, with ruined benches along the side walls. It is very similar in size and construction to the well at Llanberis on the other side of Snowdon.

Location: At the east end of the village, just off the A470 to Betws-y-coed. Beside Moriah chapel is a lane leading up the hillside to a gate. Pass through this, and the well will be seen behind a drystone wall on the right (SH 736 525).

LLANALLGO, F*fynnon Allgo* **

Until recently Ffynnon Allgo enjoyed a tranquil, rural setting on the banks of a little stream, then along came a holiday park and now the little well is an incongruous companion to a caravan. Nevertheless this is an important site. In 1983 a Celtic stone head was found nearby, and a 'capel ffynnon' at the parish church may have been paid for by pilgrim's offerings. The well is now ruined and overgrown, but the outline of a small rectangular pool, with side benches and a flagstone floor, can be made out. The water has a faint whiff of rotten eggs due to the high sulphur content, and Samuel Lewis noted that the well was *'formerly held in high veneration for... miraculous cures'*. Although this suggests that visits had fallen out of fashion by the 1830's, he adds that the spring was *'still regarded as highly beneficial in some chronic diseases'*.

Location: Llanallgo lies on the A5025 Menai Bridge to Amlwch road. Just west of the Moelfre roundabout, there is a left hand turn to Marian-glas, and the caravan park is immediately on your right. The well lies behind the fourth caravan on the right upon entering (SH 499 848).

LLANBERIS, *Ffynnon Beris****

In contrast to the rather sad condition of Ffynnon Allgo, St Peris's well is in a good state of preservation and forms a feature of the gardens of Ty'n-Ffynnon house. It is almost identical in size and form to the above well, consisting of a rectangular enclosure about 2m across, with side benches and a square pool in the flagstone floor. Everything is built from the natural slate that outcrops through the mountains of Snowdon, and which brought industrial wealth to the area in the nineteenth century. Although the pool seems rather small and shallow, it was used for immersion by patients seeking cures from rheumatism, scrofula and rickets. The church records for 1776 mention that a wooden box had been made to collect offerings from *'strangers that now and then come to a virtuous well that is in this parish'*, but by 1814 the sum was considered to be 'trifling'. From at least the end of the eighteenth century small fish used to be kept in the pool, and it was considered a sure sign of recovery if they appeared when the patient was bathing. The *Liverpool Mercury* ran a story in November 1896 claiming that two new fishes had been put in the well, to replace the one that had died the previous August. It was fifty years old, measured 48cm, and was buried with reverence in the adjoining garden.

Location: The old village lies on the A4086 about 3km beyond the tourist centre of Llanberis, in the direction of Betws-y-Coed. As you pass through the village there is a left turn just opposite a car park and facility area. Take this turn and walk towards a temporary campsite, and the well will be seen against a rock outcrop in the garden of a whitewashed house on the right. Ask permission at the house to visit it (SH 608 584).

Ffynnon Beris, Llanberis

LLANDDWYN ISLAND, *St Dwynwen's well* **

Only at exceptional tides is Llanddwyn 'island' encircled by the sea, but its coastal location was sufficiently remote for Dwynwen to live out her days in contemplation and solitude. Her name and reputation as the patron saint of lovers has lasted for centuries, and St Dwynwen's day on 25th January is still celebrated in parts of the country. According to the story she was seduced and abandoned by her lover, and retired to the island begging God to help her forget her heartache. Even her death has a sadly romantic tinge to it. As she rested in the shadow of a great boulder, she wished to see the sun set over the western sea one last time, and the rock conveniently split apart at her dying request. This miraculous spy-hole is still there today. Pilgrimages to the shrine continued through the Middle Ages, and her humble chapel was rebuilt on a grand scale in the early-sixteenth century. The shattered walls still remain on the island but, alas, the well has not been so fortunate. There is even doubt about its location; some say it was in a hollow close to the church, others that it is the spring on the cliffs beyond the split rock. The well may even have lain in the sand dunes 2km away, where OS maps mark *crochan* (cauldron) *Llanddwyn*. Wherever it was, people came to take the water to cure heartaches and *'the ravages of love'* as Samuel Lewis puts it. There was also said to be an eel living in the well, which was 'consulted' about love-matters. Breadcrumbs were scattered on the surface and a handkerchief spread on top; if the eel took the cloth along with the crumbs, it was a sign that the intended partner would be unfaithful. This story of prophetic fish is also told about the wells at Llanberis and Llangybi.

Location: From the village of Newborough on the A4080, a road leads to the Warren nature reserve. There is a car park and picnic area by the beach, and Llanddwyn Island can be reached on foot (SH 386 627).

LLANDWROG, *Ffynnon Edliw* *

Although on private land, this little spring is worth a mention for it is one of the very few survivors of a number of holy wells in the Caernarfon area - though for how much longer? Already the farmer has been dumping earth and stones close by, and so it may not be long before Ffynnon Edliw is gone for good. On the edge of a small wood (named after the well) a copious spring flows out of a small, stone lined chamber, roofed over with a flat slab.

Location: On enclosed farmland about 7.5km along the A499 from Caernarfon to Clynnog Fawr. The well lies in the bottom of a field opposite a layby and AA telephone, close by the entrance to Glynllifon College (SH 449 554).

The ruins of St Dwynwen's Church on Llanddwyn Island

Ffynnon Edliw, Llandwrog

LLANEILIAN, ***Ffynnon Eilian*** **

Like the better-known site at Llanelian-yn-rhos, this Ffynnon Eilian also had a dark reputation for bringing bad luck upon people. Scratching someone's name on a piece of slate and dropping it in the water inflicted curses. A more cruel ritual performed here involved carefully skewering a frog with a thin metal spike, placing corks on the pointed ends, and letting the unfortunate amphibian float on the water. The recipient of the curse was supposed to suffer for as long as the frog lived.

However, this was not wholly an 'evil' site; in fact, more people would come here to place blessings on crops and cattle, or to seek cures from scrofula, fits, and the palsy. It was such a popular venue that the churchwardens were able to purchase two local farms with the contributions left by visitors, and then use the rents to pay for the upkeep of the parish church. Ffynnon Eilian lies down by the sea, *'among wild and broken rocks'*, as Samuel Lewis puts it, in the shade of a rocky outcrop. It is now almost dry, but a little water trickles out of a crevice and flows across the floor of a crudely-built rectangular structure about 3.5m by 3.9m. This looks like a bathing pool, but Lewis adds that, after drinking the water, pilgrims would *'kneel for some time before the altar of a small chapel erected over* [the well]'. From this it would appear that Ffynnon Eilian was a small well-chapel, like St Govans or Capel Trillo, and it may also have had a vaulted roof. Although only the overgrown footings remain today, the coastal setting is superb and well worth the walk on a fine day.

Location: The well lies next to a waymarked coastal path along the north-east coast of Anglesey. There is parking by Porth Eilian beach, which lies past the village of Llaneilian, 2.5km east of Amlwch. Follow the path westwards for about 1.2km, to a small bay crossed by a stream, & the well will be found against a rock outcrop (SH 466 934).

LLANGELYNIN, ***Ffynnon Gelynin******

Hidden away in the mountains high above the Conwy valley, and with only isolated farms for neighbours, Llangelynin has a setting few other churches in Wales can rival. The small and austere building hides a surprising interior graced with wall paintings and inscriptions, all roofed over with a forest of dark oak beams. The foundations of a round hut can be traced in the long grass just south of the churchyard - could this have been the humble Dark Age home of St Celynin? Nearby is a ruined inn where mountain travellers could slake their thirst, while their more spiritual needs were satisfied by the holy well in a corner of the churchyard wall. Ffynnon Gelynin is a small, slab-lined pool of water surrounded by drystone walls. The church records of 1739 described it as *'a fine Spring-well, and ye House above it is... in good repair'*. It originally had a slate roof.

The water was used for baptisms in the church and for healing sick children. After being dipped in the well the infants were carried to a nearby farmhouse to recover. If worried parents wanted to foresee the outcome, they would place an item of the child's clothing on the water; if it floated, all would be well, but if it sank, the signs were bad.

Francis Jones referred to another spring nearby which was claimed to cure warts. However, in contrary to the usual practice the sufferer had to drop a pin in before washing or, not only would the wart fail to heal, but the patient would catch the warts of everyone else who had used the well before!

Location: The church lies about 5km south-west of Conwy, and can best be reached by following the B5106 out of the town towards Dolgarrog for about 2.5km, then taking the signposted right turn. Cross over the Gyffin river, and follow the signs up into the mountains. The way is narrow and twisting. There is a small parking area beyond the last gate, and a short walk brings you to the church (SH 751 737).

Llangelynin; Ffynnon Gelynin lies behind the wall in the foreground

LLANRHOS WELL

Virtually nothing is known about this little well, no traditions are recorded about it, and the diligent Francis Jones missed it. Nevertheless the character of the rough stonework suggests it is very old. The clear water rises in a semi-circular recess in a hollow, and is roofed over with a flat slab stone. Several steps lead down to the spring, and the whole site has been carefully landscaped in recent years. Perhaps the well was dedicated (like the church) to St Mary, and would have been an essential source of water for this rocky parish. There is a sixth-century memorial stone in the church where, according to legend, the contemporary ruler Maelgwn Gwynedd (whose stronghold was at nearby Deganwy castle) hid to avoid being killed by a monster.

Location: Llanrhos lies next to the B5115 road from Conwy to Llandudno. Opposite the church turn into a cul-de-sac named Cae-rhos, and walk through the gate at the end of the lane to the well (SH 792 803).

THE LLEYN PENINSULA

The 'Land's End' of north Wales stretches like an arm into the Irish Channel, pointing to the rocky island of Enlli, fabled resting place of 20,000 saints. Such was the sanctity of this remote site that numerous pilgrims endured the long and arduous trek to St Mary's abbey, and their offerings contributed to the upkeep of many churches and shrines along the way. It is no surprise that holy wells come thick and fast as the peninsula narrows to its western extremity. The RCAHMW lists some two dozen wells in Lleyn, and Francis Jones gives a total of thirty-eight. Some are marked on OS maps, but only a few have any associated buildings or structures remaining. The following seven are the best and most accessible on the peninsula.

The first reached from the direction of Caernarfon is at Clynnog Fawr (SH 413 494), a little village dominated by an exceptionally grand early-sixteenth century church. **Ffynnon Beuno** can be found next to the A499, just outside the village, and consists of an open pool in a square enclosure measuring 2.6m by 3.9m, with steps descending into the water. Patients would immerse themselves in the well, then sleep the night away on the rush-strewn tomb of St Beuno in the church. Thomas Pennant once saw a feather bed on the tomb, on which *'a poor paralytic from Meironeddshire had lain the whole night'*(1781). The water was also mixed with plaster scraped from the pillars, and applied as a paste to cure sore eyes. Whether this was ever effective is debatable, but the damage done to the building inevitably caused the church authorities much concern.

Ffynnon Beuno (Chris Barber)

The next village reached is Llanaelhearn (SH 385 447), nestling in the shadow of the three peaks of Yr Eifl. On the left hand side of the road to Nefyn is a small, grim-looking building constructed in 1900 over **Ffynnon Aelhearn**, to protect the water supply. Prior to this the well was an open pool like Clynnog. Patients would wait for the 'troubling of the waters' (when bubbles break the surface) before immersing themselves. The nearby church contains a gravestone commemorating a fifth century settler from Yorkshire. Further along the A499 to Pwlhelli a minor road to Llanarmon and Llangybi branches off to the left. This passes close to Llyn Glasfryn, where **Ffynnon Grasi** (SH 404 423) breaks out from a tangle of undergrowth and tumbled stonework on the lakeside. According to legend a woman named Grasi forgot to put the lid back on the well one night, and the water overflowed and formed the lake. Sir John Rhys collected several tales of the negligent lady in his *'Celtic Folklore'* (1901).

From here there are several ways to reach the most famous well in Lleyn (indeed, one of the most famous in all Wales), and there are plenty of signs to guide the way through the twisting lanes to **Ffynnon Gybi** (SH 427 413). A path leads past Llangybi church (note the Dark Age cross beside the gate) and down the valley to the holy well.

Ffynnon Gybi, Llangybi; the well building is on the left,
with the ruins of a later cottage adjoining.

Plan & reconstruction of Ffynnon Gybi

St Cybi created the well by striking the ground with his staff, although this miracle is also claimed to have taken place at his main ecclesiastical centre at Holyhead. By the eighteenth century so many people were taking the waters to cure blindness, scrofula, rheumatism and lameness, that the landowner was persuaded to improve the facilities. He built a small cottage where patients would rest after bathing twice daily in the well. The course of treatment could last up to ten days.

All is now in ruins. The cottage can be identified easily enough by the windows and tottering chimney. Architectural details suggest that the little dwelling was added to a free-standing well building of uncertain (perhaps medieval) date. This is roughly constructed from massive boulders, forming a rectangular chamber 3.6m by 4.4m, with rounded external corners, and a bathing pool in the centre of the flagstone floor. The water rises in an adjoining chamber and fills the pool, before draining away to the river.

From here continue on the A499 through Pwllheli, and then branch off at Llanbedrog for the B4413 to Aberdaron. After 2km detour left to Mynytho (SH 309 309) and take the lower road through the village. Beside Horeb chapel is a narrow which brings you to **Ffynnon Fyw** (*the living well*) or - according to Samuel Lewis- Ffynnon Duw (*God's well*). An old chapel dedicated to St Curig once stood nearby and it may be that the well was originally dedicated to this saint. This is one of the most substantial holy wells surviving in Wales today, although it has become a little ruinous and overgrown since it was last restored in 1959. The well is constructed from large rounded boulders, and forms a walled enclosure 4.8m square. There are two pools in the flagstone floor reached by stone steps, and the smaller one was intended for drinking, while the larger and deeper pool was used for bathing. There is a tradition that the well cured blindness, and that the healing water only rises on alternate years.

Continue along the main road to Aberdaron and take the left-hand turn to the village of Bryncroes, (SH 226314) where **Ffynnon Fair** can easily be found beside the road. This is another open pool structure like Clynnog, although the masonry has been restored in more recent times. Samuel Lewis mentioned that *'an ancient chapel, called Ty Fair '* stood nearby. There are several small wells on the slopes of Mynydd Rhiw a few kilometres to the south, and Sir John Rhys recorded an odd tradition about one of them. Wart sufferers had to travel to and from the spring without talking to anyone or looking back and, after rubbing the wart with a greasy rag, had to hide the cloth under a stone in order to achieve a cure.

An equally bizarre ritual is associated with the last of the Lleyn wells. If you take a mouthful of water from **Ffynnon Fair** near Aberdaron

Ffynnon Fyw, Myntho; the small pool on the left
was used for drinking and the larger one for bathing

(SH 139 252), and succeed in walking around the ruined chapel of St Mary -without dribbling- then your wish will be fulfilled. However, all is not as simple as it sounds; the well is a natural spring among the rocks at sea level, while the chapel is at the end of a steep and tricky climb up the hill-side! The spring rises in a basin under an overhanging crag, and is said to give a flow of pure water once the tide has retreated (although on my visit it tasted decidedly briny). Of the chapel only the foundations can be seen in a field beside the National Trust car park at the end of a minor road from Aberdaron. Here, at the very tip of the Lleyn peninsula, weary pilgrims could gaze across the short, but treacherous stretch of water separating them from their goal, and offer up a prayer for a safe crossing to the sacred isle of Enlli.

Location: All the wells described are accessible except for Ffynnon Grasi, and should be easily located. There are numerous signs pointing the way to Llangybi off the A497 Criccieth road, and the A499 from Clynnog. For Ffynnon Fair, follow the signs from Aberdaron (B4413) to Uwchmynydd, and continue past the little village to the end of the road. The well is down in the gulley between the two hills.

PENMON, ***St Seriol's well*** ***

According to legend St Seriol and St Cybi would leave their respective churches at Penmon and Holyhead, and meet up once a week at Clorach in the centre of Anglesey. There the travellers refreshed themselves at two holy wells which, in time, became named after them. Cybi faced the sun on his outward and return journeys and was nicknamed 'the bronzed', but poor Seriol 'the pale' had his back to the sun both ways! Very little remains of the Dark Age ecclesiastical settlement at Penmon, for it was later refounded as an Augustinian priory, and the present buildings date from the twelfth century onwards.

In a walled enclosure behind the austere priory church is a little group of buildings sheltering unobtrusively against a rock outcrop. One of them is a small circular hut which tradition identifies as St Cybi's humble dwelling. The age and function of this building has been criticised by CADW: Welsh Historic Monuments in a recent guidebook, but there seems no reason why it should not be early. The well itself rises in a vaulted chamber 1.8m square with a flagstone floor and several wall recesses. The brick vault and upper walls were built in the early-eighteenth century, and so presumably the well was originally an open pool. In front of it is a larger courtyard with side benches, where pilgrims would wait their turn to make their ablutions in the spring. Apart from the brickwork, all the masonry is likely to be medieval and was probably built long before the Reformation closed the priory in 1538. The healing quality of the spring was well known, and at the end of the nineteenth century the Rev Elias Owen was introduced to a man who, many years before, had gone at night to fetch water for his sick friend. Although on his deathbed the patient drank the water, recovered, and lived on for another forty years.

Location: Behind the priory at Penmon at the south-east tip of Anglesey. There is ample parking and the way is signposted from Beaumaris, via the A545 from Menai Bridge (SH 630 807).

St Seriol's Well, Penmon (Chris Barber)

St Seriol's Well, Penmon

St Gwenfaen's Well, Rhoscolyn

RHOSCOLYN, ***St Gwenfaen's Well*** ***

'Full oft have I repaired to drink that spring, waters which cure diseases of the soul as well as body', wrote the eighteenth century poet Lewis Morris. Next to Penmon, this is the most elaborate holy well surviving in Anglesey, and has one of the finest settings of any in Wales. Ffynnon Wenfaen lies about 1km away from the parish church, on a low coastal headland at the southernmost tip of Holyhead. Perhaps the invigorating walk needed to reach the well contributed to the cures, for Ffynnon Wenfaen was particularly renowned for curing depression and mental illness. Two white quartz pebbles used to be thrown in as an offering after drinking the water, a custom surely derived from the saint's name - wen faen = white stone.

The ancient-looking well is roughly built of lichen covered boulders, and forms a sunken forecourt about 1.8m square, with stone benches in each corner. From here steps lead down into a small, semi-circular chamber filled with clear spring water, which trickles away down to the sea.

Location: From the A5 at Valley, cross the causeway towards Treaddur, and then branch off along a signposted road to Rhoscolyn. Park by the church and walk along the public footpath past a farm to the coastguard station on the headland. Once there, turn right and follow a well-worn path between the sea and field wall. The well will be reached after about 500m (SH 259 754).

TREFRIW WELLS ***

When Lewis Morris praised the virtuous waters of St Gwenfaen's Well, no-one had ever heard of a medicinal spring at Trefriw. Another eighty-odd years were to pass before the particularly potent mineral qualities of this spring came to the attention of Victorian health addicts. This was the last spa to open in Wales and, according to T. R. Roberts (*The Spas of Wales* 1897), it was discovered by a mine agent in 1833 whilst surveying for potential sites. A local man had told the agent about an old 'sulphur mine' in the hillside above the Conwy valley, and when the blocked tunnel was reopened, the chalybeate water flowed out. There is a lingering belief that the original mine was dug by the Romans, but there does not seem to be any firm evidence of this, although there is a Roman fort a few kilometres away. The landowner later decided to exploit the iron-rich water and constructed a bath house at the entrance to the mine in the 1860's. This is still here today - a grim, forbidding structure built from monolithic chunks of slate. Water was brought down from the mine and used to fill two huge slate baths inside, although later one of the rooms was turned into a single large bathing pool.

Victorian pumphouse at the entrance to Trefiw Wells (Chris Barber)

Around 1900 the increasing popularity of the spa led to the addition of a large pump house at the entrance to the spa. Visitors would stay in the nearby village and travel by horse and carriage for their daily treatment, or else would arrive by boat from Conwy town. When the popular steamer trips along the river ceased in the 1930's, trade dwindled away, and Trefriw fell into decay like the other spas. However, within recent years Trefriw has witnessed a resurgence as the medicinal qualities of the chalybeate water have been marketed world-wide. The main building now contains a museum and gift shop, and visitors can sample the appallingly rich iron water direct from the mine where it flows out of dark tunnels dripping with ferrous stalactites.

Location: Trefriw Wells lies next to the B5106 Betws-y-coed to Conwy road, about 2km north of Trefriw village, and is open most days of the year (SH 778 652).

WAUN, ***Ffynnon Cegin Arthur****

The name of this chalybeate spring literally translates as the 'well of King Arthur's kitchen', but some scholars have suggested that *cegin*, in this context, refers to a nearby rocky ridge, rather than the usual sense of a kitchen. According to T R Roberts (*The Spas of Wales*, 1897), this well was so popular that carriages ran twice a day from the nearby town of Port Dinorwic. The iron-rich water was considered good for rheumatism, and a course of treatment lasted up to three weeks. There is no trace of the well today (despite still being marked on OS maps), only the ruins of the custodian's cottage in a conifer plantation. However, an adjacent drainage ditch appears to have diverted the spring, since the water has the usual reddish sediment of chalybeate.

Location: From Caernarfon take the A4086 to Llanberis and just past the village of Llanrug take the left turn to Penisaír Waun. Continue along for about 1.5km and take the left turn to Llanddeiniolen. After a short distance turn right past Tai Arthur along a dead-end road, and park by the gate in the forestry. A public footpath leads off the left side of the road. Follow this until it is crossed by a little stream. The site of the well is in the trees on the right (SH 555 648).

REFERENCES & FURTHER READING

The principal source for anyone researching this subject is, of course, Francis Jones' *The Holy Wells of Wales* (University of Wales Press 1954). A more readable and up-to-date book is *Sacred Waters* by Janet & Colin Bord (Granada 1985). Although only 24 Welsh sites are included, the book contains numerous photographs of wells elsewhere in Britain, and details of the widespread beliefs and traditions associated with them. As well as the sources mentioned in the main text, further information can be gleaned from the following books and journals.

Archaeologia Cambrensis Yearly journal published by the Cambrian Archaeological Association.

F Alderson — *The Inland Resorts and Spas of Britain* (David & Charles 1973)

Richard Fenton — *Tours in Wales* (1804-13), *A Historical Tour through Pembrokeshire* (1811)

Wendy Davies — *Wales in the Early Middle Ages* (University of Leicester Press 1982)

G T Jones & T Roberts — *Place-names of Anglesey* (Anglesey County Council 1996)

Edward Lhuyd — *Parochalia* (c1697, reprinted in Archaeologia Cambrensis 1909-11)

Samuel Lewis — *Topographical Dictionary of Wales* 1833 (1840 edition used here)

Thomas Pennant — *Tours in Wales* 1778 & 1781.(Caernarfon 1883 edition)

John Rhys, — *Celtic Folklore* (Oxfordshire Press 1901)

T R Roberts — *The Spas of Wales* (London 1897)

Royal Commission on Ancient & Historic Monuments in Wales (RCAHM) *Inventories of the Counties of Anglesey* (1937), *Caernarfon* (1956,í60,í64), *Carmarthen* (1917), *Denbigh* (1912), *Flint* (1912), *Meirioneth* (1921), *Montgomery* (1911), Pembrokeshire *(1925)*, & Radnor *(1913)*.

Paul Davis was born and bred in the Rhondda, educated at Ysgol Gyfun Rhydfelen and Dyfed College of Art. He has worked as an illustrator with the Dyfed Archaeological Trust as is now a surveyor working in Cardiff. Other publications include: *Historic Rhondda, Castles of the Welsh Princes, Historic Gower, Historic Inns and Taverns of Wales and the Marches,* and *A Company of Forts.*